S. HRG. 114–407

FIRSTNET OVERSIGHT: AN UPDATE ON THE STATUS OF THE PUBLIC SAFETY BROADBAND NETWORK

HEARING

BEFORE THE

SUBCOMMITTEE ON COMMUNICATIONS, TECHNOLOGY, INNOVATION, AND THE INTERNET

OF THE

COMMITTEE ON COMMERCE, SCIENCE, AND TRANSPORTATION UNITED STATES SENATE

ONE HUNDRED FOURTEENTH CONGRESS

SECOND SESSION

JUNE 21, 2016

Printed for the use of the Committee on Commerce, Science, and Transportation

U.S. GOVERNMENT PUBLISHING OFFICE

22–358 PDF   WASHINGTON : 2016

For sale by the Superintendent of Documents, U.S. Government Publishing Office
Internet: bookstore.gpo.gov   Phone: toll free (866) 512–1800; DC area (202) 512–1800
Fax: (202) 512–2104   Mail: Stop IDCC, Washington, DC 20402–0001

SENATE COMMITTEE ON COMMERCE, SCIENCE, AND TRANSPORTATION

ONE HUNDRED FOURTEENTH CONGRESS

SECOND SESSION

JOHN THUNE, South Dakota, *Chairman*

ROGER F. WICKER, Mississippi	BILL NELSON, Florida, *Ranking*
ROY BLUNT, Missouri	MARIA CANTWELL, Washington
MARCO RUBIO, Florida	CLAIRE McCASKILL, Missouri
KELLY AYOTTE, New Hampshire	AMY KLOBUCHAR, Minnesota
TED CRUZ, Texas	RICHARD BLUMENTHAL, Connecticut
DEB FISCHER, Nebraska	BRIAN SCHATZ, Hawaii
JERRY MORAN, Kansas	EDWARD MARKEY, Massachusetts
DAN SULLIVAN, Alaska	CORY BOOKER, New Jersey
RON JOHNSON, Wisconsin	TOM UDALL, New Mexico
DEAN HELLER, Nevada	JOE MANCHIN III, West Virginia
CORY GARDNER, Colorado	GARY PETERS, Michigan
STEVE DAINES, Montana	

NICK ROSSI, *Staff Director*
ADRIAN ARNAKIS, *Deputy Staff Director*
REBECCA SEIDEL, *General Counsel*
JASON VAN BEEK, *Deputy General Counsel*
KIM LIPSKY, *Democratic Staff Director*
CHRIS DAY, *Democratic Deputy Staff Director*
CLINT ODOM, *Democratic General Counsel and Policy Director*

———

SUBCOMMITTEE ON COMMUNICATIONS, TECHNOLOGY, INNOVATION, AND THE INTERNET

ROGER F. WICKER, Mississippi, *Chairman*	BRIAN SCHATZ, Hawaii, *Ranking*
ROY BLUNT, Missouri	MARIA CANTWELL, Washington
MARCO RUBIO, Florida	CLAIRE McCASKILL, Missouri
KELLY AYOTTE, New Hampshire	AMY KLOBUCHAR, Minnesota
TED CRUZ, Texas	RICHARD BLUMENTHAL, Connecticut
DEB FISCHER, Nebraska	EDWARD MARKEY, Massachusetts
JERRY MORAN, Kansas	CORY BOOKER, New Jersey
DAN SULLIVAN, Alaska	TOM UDALL, New Mexico
RON JOHNSON, Wisconsin	JOE MANCHIN III, West Virginia
DEAN HELLER, Nevada	GARY PETERS, Michigan
CORY GARDNER, Colorado	
STEVE DAINES, Montana	

(II)

CONTENTS

FIRSTNET OVERSIGHT: AN UPDATE ON THE STATUS OF THE PUBLIC SAFETY BROADBAND NETWORK

TUESDAY, JUNE 21, 2016

U.S. SENATE,
SUBCOMMITTEE ON COMMUNICATIONS, TECHNOLOGY,
INNOVATION, AND THE INTERNET,
COMMITTEE ON COMMERCE, SCIENCE, AND TRANSPORTATION,
Washington, DC.

The subcommittee met, pursuant to notice, at 9:33 a.m. in room SR–253, Russell Senate Office Building, Hon. Roger Wicker, Chairman of the Subcommittee, presiding.

Present: Senators Wicker [presiding], Schatz, Gardner, Daines, Fischer, Klobuchar, Blumenthal, Ayotte, Heller, and Manchin.

OPENING STATEMENT OF HON. ROGER F. WICKER, U.S. SENATOR FROM MISSISSIPPI

Senator WICKER. Good morning. I'm glad to convene today's hearing with my friend and colleague Ranking Member Schatz.

We would like to focus on the progress FirstNet has made and the challenges that lie ahead in deploying a nationwide public safety network. The First Responder Network Authority, also known as FirstNet, was established under the Middle Class Tax Relief and Job Creation Act of 2012. It is intended to address communication failures that slowed recovery efforts during major national emergencies, including the 9/11 attacks and Hurricane Katrina.

In Mississippi, we saw firsthand the consequences of communication network breakdown. FEMA, Red Cross, and others were hindered from providing the emergency recovery services needed during and after Katrina.

Tasked with building and operating a Nationwide Public Safety Broadband Network, the 2012 Act allocated $7 billion from spectrum auction proceeds to launch FirstNet. The AWS–3 spectrum auction, which concluded in January 2015, raised the $7 billion needed to begin the planning and development stage.

Although FirstNet has made commendable progress in the first year, questions linger about the future viability of the network. I appreciate FirstNet's commitment to providing our rural communities with the same services as larger urban cities, but rural and remote coverage remains a major concern of mine.

The cost of coverage and maintenance of the network in these hard-to-reach areas needs to be addressed on the front end of deployment. An accurate inventory of towers and equipment is critical to ensuring that infrastructure is capable of withstanding 200-mile-per-hour winds during storms similar to Katrina.

Each region of the country faces a unique set of challenges, and addressing these challenges is critical to fulfilling Congress's goal of creating FirstNet. We should ensure that FirstNet's plan for deployment includes the technical requirements that may be necessary.

However, we recognize that nationwide deployment will not occur overnight. Over the next several months, FirstNet will be reviewing bids to award a contract for all aspects of deployment. As this process moves forward, I urge FirstNet and all stakeholders to look carefully at the long-term viability of the network.

With a limited user base, FirstNet must have the sophistication to determine who has not only the technical capacity, but also the ability to monetize the network in order to keep it running in the future. The costs placed on public safety entities to use the network are also a major concern with regard to long-term sustainability.

Last year's oversight hearing examined the progress that had been made and FirstNet's plan for outreach to stakeholders in each State and territory. Today, I look forward to hearing about FirstNet's accomplishment in the past year, what benchmarks have been met, and what work still needs to be done.

I want to welcome all of our witnesses and thank them for testifying this morning. Our panel today includes a number of stakeholders overseeing the deployment process who can help shed light on the challenges ahead.

Senator Schatz.

STATEMENT OF HON. BRIAN SCHATZ, U.S. SENATOR FROM HAWAII

Senator SCHATZ. Thank you, Mr. Chairman. And thank you to our witnesses. I especially want to offer my welcome to Hawaii's Adjutant General, General Logan.

We are here today to discuss the progress FirstNet has made toward creating an interoperable nationwide wireless broadband network for first responders. In 2012, when Congress created FirstNet, we made an important commitment to public safety. The new Federal entity we created is a unique public-private partnership mandated to deploy this network for first responders. At the time this legislation was passed, we still lacked a nationwide interoperable public safety communication network in spite of the glaring communications problems that had been exposed following the tragedies of September 11th and Hurricane Katrina.

Until this network is built, our first responders will have to carry their bulky land mobile radios for their mission-critical voice communications and carry around a commercial smartphone for their data needs. There is really no reason that a 16-year-old with a smartphone should have more technology at their fingertips than our first responders.

FirstNet will provide first responders mission-critical data use for the first time. This network will be built and hardened to public safety specifications. It will have rugged eyes and competitive devices and specific public safety applications. For example, firefighters could download the blueprint of a burning building before they enter; a police officer arriving at the scene can run a background check or get pictures of a suspect by accessing a Federal law enforcement database; most importantly, emergency personnel will not be competing with commercial users for bandwidth. They will have priority on this network.

FirstNet's staff and board should be congratulated for releasing its RFP earlier this year, which is a real milestone toward construction of the network. They have received bids and will be evaluating potential vendors during the next several months while continuing to work with states on their participation. As they progress, FirstNet and its commercial partner will have to make sure that first responders and each State sees the value in the network.

As General Logan may touch upon today, we need to ensure that the specific needs of all states and territories are respected in order to accommodate for geographic and other differences across our great country.

While Congress will continue to keep a close eye on FirstNet's work, the reality is that we are in a wait-and-see mode until FirstNet chooses its private sector partner, and so I expect that Mr. Poth may not be able to address every issue raised today, as they are in the middle of a procurement process. Once the vendor has been chosen, FirstNet and all of its partners can begin in earnest to build the network that delivers on the promise that Congress made to public safety in 2012.

Again, I want to thank the witnesses for appearing before the Committee, and I look forward to hearing your testimony.

Senator WICKER. Thank you, Senator Schatz. Our witnesses today are Mr. Michael Poth, CEO of FirstNet; Mr. Jeffrey McLeod, Director of Homeland Security and Public Safety Division of the National Governors Association; Senator Schatz has already mentioned Major General Arthur J. Logan, the Single Point of Contact, State of Hawaii, and the Hawaii Adjutant General; and, fourthly, Mr. Andrew Katsaros, Assistant Inspector General for Audit, U.S. Department of Commerce, Washington, D.C.

Gentlemen, we appreciate all of you being with us today, and we'll begin with the testimony of Mr. Poth and ask each of you if you could limit your verbal testimony to 5 minutes. Thank you.

Mr. Poth.

STATEMENT OF MICHAEL POTH, CHIEF EXECUTIVE OFFICER, FIRST RESPONDER NETWORK AUTHORITY (FirstNet)

Mr. POTH. Thank you, Chairman Wicker, Ranking Member Schatz, and Members of the Subcommittee. Thank you for inviting me to testify today.

Since I began at FirstNet a little over 10 months ago, I've seen firsthand the dedication that the FirstNet board and staff have toward the successful deployment of the nationwide public safety broadband network. Public safety, that's who we work for every day, and we have never taken our focus off the goal of delivering the best possible network for the men and women who keep us safe and put themselves in harm's way every single day. We are the stewards for their network.

I'd like to take just a moment and thank those public safety personnel who are in the audience today. Senators, their presence are an indication that they are keeping all of our feet to the fire as we work together in making FirstNet a reality.

We've accomplished a great deal over the past 12 months: wrapped up our initial consultation meetings with every State and territory partner who requested one; kicked off 2016 consultation with our single points of contacts meetings, SPOCs; and are well underway in the State governance board meetings in coordination with our SPOCs. Then we released the RFP and are now moving forward aggressively toward award.

It is around the RFP that I would like to focus the majority of my comments today. When the FirstNet chairwoman, Sue Swenson, testified before the full committee around 15 months ago, she laid out the roadmap that FirstNet was planning to move along in order to successfully conduct consultation with the states and develop a procurement strategy that would ultimately result in a public-private partnership with the vendor. FirstNet continues to honor our commitments to do what we set out to do on time and under budget.

We have to ensure not only that our 16 core objectives, including rural build-out, cybersecurity, public safety adoption, and financial sustainability, could be met by the vendor community, but we had to propose a business opportunity model that would ultimately be a win for public safety, a win for the states, a win for FirstNet, and a win for our commercial partner: a true public-private partnership across the board.

Based on what we've seen in the past, the financial incentive was not enough for the commercial community to do this on their own, and we know that the taxpayer funds are simply not there to do this by ourselves. In essence, we had to develop a business proposition that fulfilled the needs of both parties. In developing the RFP, we met with hundreds of commercial entities, educating them on the business proposition, listening to their concerns, while trying to establish best methods and bringing the commercial world to the table.

We're in the marketing mode to create the demand. In the build-up to the release, FirstNet held numerous industry days, informational sessions with the investment community, educational webinars for the vendor community, and public speaking engagements on both the draft RFP documents and the final RFP.

Ultimately, after a year of intense work, we were able to release the RFP back in January of this year. The RFP was open to the vendor community for a little over 5 months, and was closed on this May 31st. We are confident that the RFP will lead to the successful public-private partnership that Congress envisioned.

We're also confident the value proposition we have put forward will enable our partner to achieve the public safety user adoption targets, the coverage goals, the price points, and financial sustainability that we need. We will maximize the value of the $7 billion and the 20 megahertz spectrum that Congress and the American taxpayer provided FirstNet.

We also know that the public safety user base exists, and "user adoption targets" will become a contract term. We have designed the RFP to incentivize our partner to achieve the goals, and so we are allowing the market to work in both our and public safety's advantage. We have structured financial safeguards and operational oversight controls over our partner to ensure that we have the ability to keep them accountable throughout the duration of the contract.

Today, we are in the evaluation phase of the project. Due to the rules that the Federal Acquisition Regulations, or FAR, places on FirstNet, I cannot comment on any aspects of the current actions of the organization related to the procurement.

In 2016, we still continue consultation efforts with the States, conduct outreach with State, local, tribal, and Federal public safety agencies. We will select the partner from the procurement phase of the project and begin development of the State plans. Our previously established partnerships with the states will be critical for this phase of the effort.

While we are proud of our efforts thus far, we cannot afford to rest for one moment. Too much work needs to be done. Public safety has long been demanding a broadband network, and now we are in reach of achieving this goal. The men and women who protect us from harm's way are counting on us to deliver the network, and we must do so for the sake of all first responders around the country. The need for this network has never been higher, and in order to meet the lofty expectations of public safety everywhere, I and the organization is committed to achieving the goals that Congress laid out for us just a few short years ago.

Thank you again for your support, and I look forward to your questions.

[The prepared statement of Mr. Poth follows:]

PREPARED STATEMENT OF MICHAEL POTH, CHIEF EXECUTIVE OFFICER, FIRST RESPONDER NETWORK AUTHORITY (FIRSTNET)

Introduction

Chairman Wicker, Ranking Member Schatz, and all Members of the Subcommittee, I would like to thank you for the opportunity to appear here today to provide an update on the progress we are making at FirstNet toward the deployment of an interoperable nationwide public safety broadband network (NPSBN). I also want to thank all of the Members of this Subcommittee who were pivotal in creating FirstNet. We look forward to your continued support and to working with the Subcommittee and full Committee as FirstNet moves forward with our vital mission to improve public safety's access to broadband wireless communications across the country.

Progress Toward a Network

FirstNet intends to provide cutting-edge, prioritized, and preemptive wireless broadband communications to millions of first responders at the local, state, tribal, and Federal levels across all states, territories and the District of Columbia, consistent with the vision laid out in the Middle Class Tax Relief and Job Creation Act of 2012 (P.L. 112–96) (Act). By enabling the deployment of the dedicated NPSBN, FirstNet will provide a ubiquitous solution to decades-long interoperability and communications challenges and help make our communities and first responders safer with advanced communications services, devices, and applications.

FirstNet's goal of enabling the deployment of the network and thereby meeting the needs of first responders is a matter of critical importance for public safety. Since our inception, FirstNet has taken the necessary steps to build an organization, execute a vigorous consultation and outreach strategy, develop and produce a comprehensive request for proposals (RFP), and lay the groundwork for a successful deployment of the NPSBN. Much has been accomplished. However, as it is with any such undertaking, every step forward presents new challenges, and requires that innovative solutions be identified. The past three years have involved thousands of working hours to solve the various challenges FirstNet has faced. I am proud to say that today we have an organization of people who are dedicated to public safety and to fulfilling our mission; a culture of hard work, openness, and transparency; a procurement strategy that we believe is attractive to the vendor community and will lead to a successful public-private agreement; and a robust consultation and outreach program to educate, inform, and obtain input from our stakeholders. With these accomplishments, we have sowed the seeds of success as FirstNet strives to develop the public safety broadband market here in the United States and to influence public safety around the world.

The Procurement Strategy and Development

FirstNet has engaged in an acquisition process in accordance with the Federal Acquisition Regulation (FAR). FirstNet began its market research into the development of the comprehensive RFP in early 2013. The research included meetings with vendors as well as the issuance of 13 Requests for Information (RFIs), with the last RFI and corresponding draft Statement of Objectives (SOO) released on September 17, 2014 in the form of a Special Notice. These RFIs addressed technical questions regarding the available offerings for equipment and services needed to implement the NPSBN, as well as questions regarding the acquisition approach and specific program objectives.

We developed the final RFP using information and data gathered throughout this process, as well as from our vendor meetings and "Industry Days," stakeholder consultation, and public notice processes including the release of draft RFP documents in April, 2015. Our vendor outreach program aimed to obtain a better understanding of industry's capabilities and analyzed the recommendations and alternative approaches suggested by the public to determine how to best leverage existing capabilities and best practices in order to meet public safety needs.

Following two successful "Industry Days" in 2015, FirstNet hosted a pre-proposal conference on March 10, 2016 with local participation and a simultaneous webcast. A total of 437 individuals participated representing 260 organizations, including industry, local government, media, states and territories, Federal agencies, and trade associations. The pre-proposal conference also provided key information pertaining to solicitation highlights and included upcoming key milestones and the overall phased evaluation approach contained in the solicitation.

In addition to the "Industry Days" and the pre-proposal conference, FirstNet conducted one-on-one sessions with interested vendors. These sessions were held to discuss a vendor's capabilities, current commercial offerings, and major program objectives and to learn more about industry capabilities to meet those objectives.

Through this acquisition, and the 16 objectives identified in the SOO as set forth in the solicitation, FirstNet is seeking a comprehensive network and a service solution that provides as much coverage and functionality as feasible. FirstNet's goal is to maximize the network's value to public safety while meeting our financial sustainability obligations under the Act. The objectives included in the SOO will ensure that the NPSBN operates as a single network guaranteeing seamless interoperability between states and territories, regardless of whether FirstNet or the state/territory deploys the Radio Access Network (RAN). FirstNet issued the RFP for the deployment of the NPSBN on January 13, 2016 and subsequently answered 447 industry and stakeholder questions pertaining to the solicitation and issued 14 amendments to address the questions and feedback received.

The evaluation is being conducted in a multi-phased approach. In Phase I, interested parties were given the opportunity to provide a "capability statement" demonstrating they are capable of performing the work. The submission of a capability statement afforded FirstNet the opportunity to review and evaluate the experience and capability of potential offerors while providing viable potential offerors an opportunity to receive feedback. Notifications were issued to all parties who submitted a capability statement on April 8, 2016, and feedback sessions with those determined to be viable competitors were held on April 20th and 21st.

Proposals for the comprehensive RFP were submitted by May 31, 2016. Following receipt of proposals, the Source Selection Team has commenced with the remaining evaluation phases (Phase II through Phase IV), as stated in the RFP and described below.

During Phase II, the Source Selection Team will conduct an initial review of the proposals received to verify conformance and completeness with the RFP instructions. Those proposals that have been verified as complete and conform to the RFP instructions will move into Phase III—Pass/Fail.

As stated in the RFP, under Phase III, an offeror must demonstrate its ability to sustain the annual payments to FirstNet for the life of the contract and provide coverage in each of the 56 states and territories including rural areas. Those offerors whose proposed solutions have been determined to conform to the RFP in Phase II and successfully pass Phase III will move into Phase IV. During this final phase,

FirstNet will conduct a detailed evaluation of all information and documentation received from the offerors based on the evaluation factors identified within the RFP.

FirstNet currently anticipates making an award of the NPSBN contract by November 1, 2016, although the ultimate timing is dependent on the amount of time it takes to comprehensively complete the evaluation and award process in accordance with the Federal Acquisition Regulation.

Consultation and Outreach

The consultation and outreach efforts undertaken by FirstNet over the past few years have been crucial to establishing lasting partnerships with the states, territories, tribal nations, Federal agencies, and public safety users. The information FirstNet has gathered through these efforts has informed our work to develop and deploy public safety's network and our comprehensive RFP. Consultation brings together the states and territories as partners in the development of the NPSBN by having the organization work with the State Single Point of Contacts (SPOCs) to ensure that FirstNet captures not only the needs and wishes of the local, state, and tribal public safety stakeholders, but the data that states and territories have collected through the funding provided by the National Telecommunication and Information Administration's (NTIA) State and Local Implementation Grant Program (SLIGP). Ultimately, we believe that consultation efforts will lead to the provision of better planned public safety communications services and products, and increase adoption of the NPSBN.

Initial Consultation

FirstNet's initial consultation efforts focused on working with states and territories to facilitate a forum where public safety officials could discuss real-life examples and use-cases to illustrate how the FirstNet network could be used once deployed to improve incident and emergency response. These meetings confirmed to FirstNet just how diverse and locally focused the network will need to be. States were especially eager to demonstrate how their day-to-day challenges were, in the majority of cases, unique to that particular geographic area or region. For example, the western states have vast areas of terrain that, at this point, have proven difficult, if not impossible to cover. So, the issue of rural coverage was a topic that multiple states and territories raised with FirstNet on numerous occasions.

A key takeaway from FirstNet's initial consultation efforts in 2015 was that the network is an absolute necessity and that public safety today uses significant amounts of data to carry out their duties. Time and time again, states, territories, and public safety personnel throughout the Nation emphasized the need for the network and urged that FirstNet work as quickly as possible. By the end of the initial consultation process, FirstNet had held an in-state meeting with all states and territories that had requested one.

Phase 2 Consultation

Building on the success of the initial consultation meetings, FirstNet developed a more focused second phase of consultation with the states and territories. And while FirstNet consulted with an impressive number of public safety personnel and groups during the initial consultation process, it was clear that more work needed to be done with the states and territories on the planning front. FirstNet decided to expand outreach efforts to reach a larger audience and to further educate the public safety community on our goals while concurrently focusing our consultation on individuals that will likely influence or contribute to a governor's decision on the RAN deployment to ensure such decision is informed.

FirstNet has held SPOC follow-up meetings with 54 states and territories and completed Governance Body Consultation Meetings with 18 states. These meetings are designed to connect with the states and territories on important network planning and implementation issues, such as State Plan development and a governor's decision whether to assume responsibility for RAN deployment and to have a discussion about the key influencers and key issues that the state/territory and FirstNet need to consider over the next year.

Data Collection

As part of FirstNet's consultation efforts, states collected data from local, state, territory, and tribal public safety agencies, which provided FirstNet with substantial input from public safety stakeholders across the country. This data, also collected from Federal agencies, informed our comprehensive RFP in areas such as coverage, capacity, and public safety incident locations, and this information was made available to all potential offerors. FirstNet received data from over 11,600 public safety entities representing 1.6 million public safety personnel from 54 states and territories and seven Federal agencies. We are continuing to build on that effort this year, as all states and territories that choose to do so will be able to update their information using available SLIGP funds. All data that is voluntarily collected will continue to inform FirstNet's network planning and implementation efforts.

Outreach

Throughout the consultation process, FirstNet has simultaneously engaged in extensive outreach to public safety stakeholders, including tribal communities, to educate and inform them about FirstNet and the NPSBN. As part of those efforts, FirstNet has coordinated with state and territories to support their outreach activities to public safety practitioners within their borders. FirstNet's tribal outreach team participated in the primary national and regional tribal organizations' conferences and meetings and state-hosted tribal engagements in an effort to educate tribes about FirstNet and encourage tribal participation in the state and Federal consultation and data collection process.

Federal Consultation

Although the Act focuses on engagement and planning at the state, territory, tribal, and local levels, the NPSBN will also serve public safety personnel at the Federal level. As such, FirstNet has made it a priority to consult with Federal agencies that provide public safety services to account for the needs and objectives of those potential users. FirstNet staff has conducted numerous engagements with a variety of Federal organizations across the country. FirstNet also worked closely with Federal agency points of contact to complete an initial data collection effort that we intentionally aligned with the data collection effort conducted with the states.

Tribal Outreach

FirstNet is committed to continuing its engagement with sovereign tribal nations. Tribes have a great need for the NPSBN and FirstNet's tribal outreach team have been traveling throughout the country to speak at tribal gatherings, meet with tribal nations regarding FirstNet, and support SPOC efforts to engage tribal communities

In the past two years, FirstNet's tribal outreach team participated in the primary national and regional tribal organizations' conferences and meetings and state-hosted tribal engagements in an effort to educate tribes about FirstNet and encourage tribal participation in the state and Federal consultation and data collection process.

In addition, through FirstNet's Public Safety Advisory Committee (PSAC) Tribal Working Group (TWG), FirstNet has continued to conduct regular dialogue with delegates and representatives from numerous tribal organizations.

The TWG, comprised of representatives from a broad cross-section of multi-tribal associations, was established to provide FirstNet advice on tribal outreach, education, and inclusive consultation strategies to ensure participation by tribal jurisdictions in planning for the NPSBN.

State Plans

Following the completion of the RFP process, the Act requires FirstNet to deliver a plan to each state and territory's governor. These "State Plans" will be used to guide and inform the governors on FirstNet's intended build-out of the RAN in each state or territory. The Act clearly requires the governor to decide whether FirstNet will deploy, maintain, and operate the RAN or whether the state or territory will assume such responsibility. Indeed, under the Act, until the governor makes this decision, there can be no early deployment, or any other action or decision related to the RAN in the state or territory.

Together, FirstNet and our network partner will develop all 56 State Plans. This is an enormous task given a number of factors, including: the finite resources that are available to FirstNet; the diverse and varied needs of each individual state and territory; the wide-ranging goals of the NPSBN; and public safety's expectations that FirstNet will deploy in a timely manner. To succeed in providing plans that are representative of not only the discussions that FirstNet has conducted with the states and territories, but also responsive to public safety's needs, FirstNet and our partner will need to make this process a top priority.

Following the development of draft State Plans, FirstNet plans to provide each state and territory with an opportunity to review and discuss the draft plans with FirstNet prior to the delivery of the final plan to the governor. FirstNet will strive to provide State Plans that are detailed, accurate, and comprehensive, with the information necessary for each governor to make an informed decision whether to assume responsibility for the RAN and for the Federal Communications Commission (FCC) and NTIA to perform their respective statutory responsibilities of evaluating any state or territory-proposed alternative RAN plans. States and territories have been advised that the opportunity to make wholesale changes to these plans will be minimal and the time to review will be constrained due in part to the Act's directive to speed deployment of the network.

FirstNet's goal is to deliver final State Plans to the governors in 2017. Understandably, this date must remain flexible given the time constraints and fluidity of the procurement process as well as the tight timelines that FirstNet has preliminarily established to develop all 56 State Plans with our partner post-award.

Innovative and Economic Impact of the Network

Innovation will be a hallmark of FirstNet. Not only will innovation occur at the outset of this network, it will continue in perpetuity for the benefit of public safety. If we could see into the future, five, ten, 20 years from now and beyond, I believe we would be amazed at the devices and applications that will be running on this network in support of public safety. In the commercial world we have long heard of the benefits of the Internet of Things (IOT), but imagine the benefits to public safety throughout the Nation once an "Internet of Public Safety Things" has been created. I believe that FirstNet can be that catalyst.

Several other countries are already looking to the United States and FirstNet as a model for deploying a broadband network for public safety. Australia, Canada, Mexico, South Korea, and the United Kingdom are all looking to deploy their own version of FirstNet. Just like other industries and markets, it is vital that the United States lead and be at the forefront of public safety broadband. When we lead, we grow not only our economy, but we continue to have a leading presence in global markets that will influence future generations of technology and public safety innovation.

Conclusion

I am grateful to the Subcommittee for the opportunity to update you on FirstNet's progress. As you can see, FirstNet has established an innovative business model that strikes the balance between providing public safety the network that it needs and deserves and incentivizing industry to participate in the development and deployment. FirstNet is not simply another government program. We have taken the framework provided under the Act and developed a unique startup that will leverage the best of the public safety community with the best of industry. Indeed, it is this public-private model that has driven much of our success to date and will lead to the win-win-win solution that we are striving to achieve; most importantly a win for public safety, but also a win for the private sector and a win for FirstNet.

Notwithstanding this success and all that we have accomplished in a relatively short period of time, there remains an enormous amount of work ahead. FirstNet will continue to meet our statutory obligations, partner with those who will use and benefit from the network, and work toward the successful development, deployment, and operation of the NPSBN.

I ask that this Subcommittee continue to support the organization as we move through our procurement and the selection of a network partner. I give you my commitment that FirstNet will continue to redouble our efforts in order to achieve our objectives, but we can only do so with the support of Congress, public safety, local governments, states, territories, tribal jurisdictions, Federal agencies, and our other stakeholders. Finally, it is important to remember that this is not FirstNet's network; this is public safety's network. The public safety community fought for the creation of FirstNet, and it is up to us to achieve their vision.

Senator WICKER. Thank you very much.
Mr. McLeod.

STATEMENT OF JEFFREY S. McLEOD, DIRECTOR, HOMELAND SECURITY AND PUBLIC SAFETY DIVISION, NATIONAL GOVERNORS ASSOCIATION'S CENTER FOR BEST PRACTICES

Mr. McLEOD. Chairman Wicker, Ranking Member Schatz, distinguished members of the Subcommittee, my name is Jeff McLeod. I'm Director of the Homeland Security and Public Safety Division at the National Governors Association's Center for Best Practices.

I appreciate the opportunity to appear before you as a representative of our Nation's Governors to discuss our shared commitment to building and sustaining a nationwide broadband network dedicated to public safety. NGA was a leading advocate of the public safety spectrum provisions in the legislation that led to the creation of FirstNet. NGA has represented Governors before Congress and FirstNet officials on key implementation issues and challenges facing states.

My testimony today will address factors that Governors must weigh in reaching a decision whether to join in the deployment of the public safety broadband network, as referred by FirstNet, or to opt out and take on the responsibility of deploying, operating, and maintaining a radio access network in their state.

Specifically, I'm going to focus on three issues: one, coverage; two, cost; and three, the consultation process through which FirstNet is required to engage State leaders. I would like to summarize my remarks and ask my full written testimony be submitted to the record.

Our primary consideration for Governors in reaching their decision is the network's ability to offer reliable coverage statewide. This is a top concern in states with large rural areas and in states with challenging geography. FirstNet has stated that build-out and maintenance of the network in rural areas will be funded primarily from access fees generated from the user based in more densely populated areas. Thus, they are likely to prioritize build-out in metropolitan areas before rural areas. However, the financial needs of the network must be balanced with the needs of the public safety community. State will require that the network be built out in rural areas, where commercial access is more limited.

In addition to concerns about coverage, questions of cost top the agenda for many Governors. Governors want to know, one, whether the network can be built within existing cost models; two, what the user fee to connect the network will be; and three, what are the long-term administrative and operation costs?

The financial models that underpin the network's long-term sustainability requires a robust and diverse user base. If fees are too high and public safety users do not utilize the network, the financial success of the network could be in jeopardy. States remain concerned that this could lead to user fees that exceed current outlays on public safety communications technology. Given the unprecedented nature of building and maintaining a network of this size and complexity, states are concerned about the possibility of unforeseen costs being shifted to them.

Regarding FirstNet's outreach to Governors on the consultation piece, some have expressed concern about the tone of the engagement. During the consultation process, FirstNet has referred to states as constituents. While this may appear to be mere word choice, it alters the tenor of the engagement and lessens the focus on partnership. FirstNet must view states as full partners in this endeavor. States have key information, processes, and expertise that must be brought to bear on the full range of FirstNet activities.

In closing, to many states, the opt-out scenario is a false choice. While there are a number of unknowns associated with opting in, very few states are in a position to consider taking on the unknowable and likely significant financial liabilities associated with building, operating, and maintaining, and upgrading a full radio access network in their states if they choose to opt out.

Finally, I would like to note that transition in Governors' administrations with the coming election cycles presents a continuing communication and education challenge for FirstNet.

On behalf of NGA and our members, thank you for the opportunity to testify. I look forward to any questions the Committee may have.

[The prepared statement of Mr. McLeod follows:]

PREPARED STATEMENT OF JEFFREY S. MCLEOD, DIRECTOR, HOMELAND SECURITY AND PUBLIC SAFETY DIVISION, NATIONAL GOVERNORS ASSOCIATION'S CENTER FOR BEST PRACTICES

Overview

Chairman Wicker, Ranking Member Schatz and distinguished members of the Subcommittee, my name is Jeffrey McLeod, Director of the National Governors Association's Center for Best Practices' Homeland Security and Public Safety Division. The National Governors Association (NGA) is the bipartisan organization of the Nation's governors. Through NGA, governors share best practices, speak with a collective voice on national policy, and develop innovative solutions that improve state government and support the principles of federalism.

I appreciate the opportunity to appear before you today on the implementation of the First Responder Network Authority (FirstNet). NGA was a leading advocate of the public safety spectrum provisions in the legislation that led to the creation of FirstNet, and NGA remains dedicated to implementing those provisions. Over the last four years, NGA has continued to represent governors before Congress and FirstNet officials on key implementation issues and challenges facing states. My testimony today will focus on the remaining factors governors and states must consider before reaching their respective decisions on broadband deployment.

As you may already know, governors are engaged in efforts to develop and deploy a nationwide public safety broadband network. Pursuant to FirstNet's authorizing statute, the state planning process gives governors the decision to either participate in FirstNet's deployment or follow the necessary steps to provide an alternative plan for the construction, maintenance, operation and improvements of a state radio access network.[1] That decision affects the entire state, including all individual jurisdictions.

Each state has unique needs for network coverage, which requires extensive consultation with FirstNet and other stakeholders. Although states still await FirstNet's plan for deployment, they continue to engage with FirstNet on the development of network policies and their respective plans.

Throughout the last several years of planning, states have clearly identified potential obstacles and challenges surrounding the implementation of FirstNet, primarily issues of coverage, cost and consultation. For governors, these factors are critical considerations in developing a nationwide public safety broadband network that enhances emergency response and is sustainable over the long term. My testimony today will focus on these three issues. Before I go any further, however, I would like to provide some background on the development of state plans thus far.

State Plans and Governor Decision

As I alluded to earlier, governors are faced with the decision to opt in or opt out of the FirstNet network. In the lead up to that decision, FirstNet and states have been engaging in a data collection and consultation process to prepare individual state plans. After the request for proposals (RFP) process concludes with the selection of FirstNet's commercial vendor in late 2016, state plans will be presented to governors and their state single point of contact (SPOC).

This proposal will detail FirstNet and its commercial vendor's plan for the build-out of the radio access network (RAN) within a state. Its intention is to give the governor the information he or she needs to make the decision to opt in or opt out.

Upon receiving the final plan, governors have 90 days to notify FirstNet of their decision. If they choose to opt in, there is no additional action required. FirstNet and its commercial vendor will build out the network and bear the associated cost of constructing, operating, and upgrading it. State and local first responders will then pay a user fee to access the network.[2]

[1] See 47 U.S.C. 1442(e)(2).
[2] See 47 U.S.C. 1428(a)(1).

Alternatively, governors may choose to do nothing upon receiving the state plan, letting the 90-day deadline for a decision lapse without action. According to FirstNet, this is considered de facto opt-in. Even if governors do not affirmatively opt in, they will be automatically opted into having the RAN built by FirstNet and their commercial vendor in their state.[3]

As a third option, governors may also choose to opt out of FirstNet and its commercial vendor building the RAN. In that case, governors must notify FirstNet within 90 days of receiving the plan that they plan to opt-out. Then, within 180 days, they must complete an RFP, receive any necessary legislative approval, and submit an alternative plan to the FCC. States must then submit a plan to the National Telecommunications and Information Administration (NTIA) to lease spectrum and may apply for RAN construction grant funding. Opt-out states then have to negotiate a spectrum lease with FirstNet and, finally, build out their own RAN, all within the timeframes outlined in the statute. At any point in this process, FirstNet, NTIA, or the Federal Communications Commission (FCC) can deny the state's plan to build its own RAN.[4]

States that opt out are responsible for all building, maintenance, operation and upgrade costs associated with the state RAN. Additionally, state and local users will still have to pay a fee to connect to the core FirstNet network.[5]

For many states, the opt-out scenario is a false choice. Though there are a number of unknowns associated with opting in, very few states are in a position to consider taking on the unknowable and likely significant financial liabilities associated with building, operating, maintaining, and upgrading a full RAN in their states if they opt-out.

Coverage

Going back to my three points of focus for today—coverage, cost and consultation—a primary concern for governors is the network's ability to offer sufficient and reliable coverage statewide. Specifically, they are concerned with how extensive coverage will be in rural areas and how it will differ from commercial options. This is a particular concern in states with substantial rural areas and in those with challenging geography and topography. Questions that must be adequately answered in the state plan for governors to make a fully informed decision to opt in or opt out include:

- What service will be offered in rural areas?
- When will it be offered?
- What are estimates of the cost of that service?

During the data collection phase of consultation, states provided FirstNet extensive data and maps detailing their unique coverage needs and challenges, including areas of critical concern for state and local first responders. FirstNet has said it has a duty to protect excess fees generated from densely populated areas to fund the network's buildout in rural areas. According to FirstNet, this approach ensures resources are available to build out and maintain the network in rural areas, where fees generated from the user base would otherwise be insufficient.[6] However, the financial needs of the network must be balanced with the needs of the public safety community in underserved areas.

Additionally, the FirstNet RFP outlines a number of rural buildout milestones that any commercial vendor must meet. The final milestone calls for achieving 100 percent of a vendor's proposed coverage in rural areas within five years of the contract award.[7] Including these milestones in the RFP provides evidence of FirstNet's statutorily required consideration of rural needs; however, until states have a clear understanding of what the contractor's proposed coverage looks like, the milestones are essentially meaningless. Without additional information, the milestones offer no assurances of widespread and reliable coverage.

Many states have existing contracts with commercial communication providers that offer some coverage in these areas. In the state plans, FirstNet will need to show governors that their proposed coverage provides a value-add over existing commercial options, both in terms of user cost and coverage reliability.

---

[3] Final Interpretations of Parts of the Middle Class Tax Relief and Job Creation Act of 2012, *Federal Register* 80, no. 202 (Oct. 20, 2015): 63506.

[4] *Ibid.*

[5] *Ibid.*

[6] Further Proposed Interpretations of the Parts of the Middle Class Tax Relief and Job Creation Act of 2012, *Federal Register* 80, no. 49 (Oct. 20, 2015): 13348.

[7] FirstNet Solicitation No. D15PS00295—Section J, Attachment J–8, IOC/FOC Target Timeline, (Jan. 13, 2016), 5.

Finally, states are concerned that the costs associated with building and maintaining a network with sufficient rural coverage will drive a significant increase in user fees, which will then have an impact on the rural communities that need this coverage. In building this network and structuring user fees, states must be assured that sufficient coverage will not lead to burdensome user fees for resource-scarce state and local first responders.

Costs

In addition to concerns about coverage, questions of cost top the agenda of many governors and state policymakers. Governors are concerned about (1) what the user fees to connect to the network will be; (2) whether the network can be built within existing cost models; and (3) what any long-term administrative management and operation costs may be. States understand that these questions cannot be answered at this time. However, they expect increased clarity from FirstNet and its commercial vendor before deciding whether to opt in.

Chief among states' concerns is the user fee structure. It is expected that FirstNet will reinvest user fees into maintaining and upgrading the national network. Given the size and scope of this network, supporting it will require significant financial investment throughout its lifecycle.

The financial models that underpin the network's long-term sustainability require a robust and diverse user base. If fees are too high and public safety users do not utilize the network, the financial success of the network could be in jeopardy. States remain concerned that this could lead to user fees in excess of the amount currently spent on public safety communications technology.

States and municipalities operate within constrained budgets, and user fees for this network remain largely unknown. Additionally, municipalities have vastly disparate budget requirements. In other words, what one city can afford may be far different from what another can. In particular, this affects rural communities, which frequently operate in a severely constrained budget environment.

There are also significant questions as to how the FirstNet user fees will compare with existing commercial user fees. Where commercial providers can offer a similar service at a lower cost, users will be less inclined to utilize FirstNet's services. Again, though states recognize these questions cannot be answered at this time, these concerns factor significantly into the governor's decision-making process.

Beyond user fees, governors seek further assurance that states will not incur unforeseen costs from FirstNet down the road. FirstNet has asserted that if states make the decision to opt in to the network, the costs associated with building and maintaining the network will be the sole responsibility of FirstNet and its commercial vendor. Given the unprecedented nature of building and maintaining a network of this size and complexity, states are concerned about the possibility of unforeseen costs being shifted to them. Though the costs of opting out of the network are almost certain to be greater than opting in, governors will have to consider this financial uncertainty as they weigh their decision to opt in or out.

Finally, states are also grappling with the difficulty of determining the operational and administrative costs that will be incurred by state communications agencies when operating on the FirstNet network. Operating a statewide communications network requires significant administrative and personnel costs, and this will certainly be the case when FirstNet is fully deployed. Costs may include purchasing new equipment or upgrading existing equipment to fully utilize the services offered on the network. States must consider how those costs compare with existing commercial solutions and current state systems.

Consultation and Partnership

That brings me to my last point: consultation. Throughout the mandated consultation and data collection process, FirstNet has engaged state leaders on the planned buildout of the nationwide network. However, states have had some concerns regarding the tone of this engagement. As NGA has previously emphasized, FirstNet must view states as partners in this endeavor. The reason for that is not only to meet the statutory requirements for state consultations, but more important to ensure that key information, processes and expertise within states can be appropriately brought to bear on the full range of FirstNet activities.[8]

Since 2013, FirstNet has engaged in extensive consultation with state, local, county and tribal leaders across the Nation. However, some states have described this

---

[8] Governor Martin O'Malley and Governor Mary Fallin, "FirstNet Hearing Letter to Chairman Greg Walden and the Honorable Anna Eshoo," (Mar. 13, 2013), available at: *http://www.nga.org/cms/home/federal-relations/nga-letters/homeland-security_public-safety/col2-content/main-content-list/march-13-2013-letter_firstnet.html.*

engagement as largely focused on satisfying the statutory consultation requirement, rather than developing genuine partnerships with states. Further, some states remain concerned they are viewed as mere customers of an eventual national broadband network. During the consultation process, FirstNet refers to states as "constituents." Althought this may appear to be mere word choice, it alters the tenor of the engagement and lessens the focus on partnership. For the network to succeed, states must be viewed as full-fledged partners.

Additionally, outreach to states must be done in a consistent fashion and should rely on the existing Single Point of Contact network that was developed at the outset of this process. Communication with senior state leaders outside of this framework may result in mixed messages and duplicative efforts within states. Using this network is the most effective way for FirstNet to reach governors and their senior staff. Going through these channels ensures that all the necessary information is available for governors to make their decision.

Finally, transition in gubernatorial administrations with the coming election cycles presents a communication and education challenge for FirstNet. Given the long-term timeline associated with building this network and delivering services, FirstNet should ensure it is prepared for eventual turnover in a number of governors' offices, including key homeland security, public safety, and information technology staff during the 2016, 2017 and 2018 election cycles.

Conclusion

Governors appreciate the support of this committee in ensuring progress toward implementation of a nationwide public safety broadband network. If implemented in a manner that ensures maximum coverage at a reasonable, certain, and fair cost to states, and with a consultation process focused on establishing partnerships, FirstNet has the potential to enhance the ability of first responders to protect states and localities from harm and provide timely responses to requests for emergency assistance.

On behalf of the National Governors Association and our members, thank you for the opportunity to testify. Governors and NGA stand ready to work with this committee to ensure the successful implementation and deployment of a national public safety broadband network for first responders.

Senator WICKER. Well, thank you very much.
General Logan.

STATEMENT OF MAJOR GENERAL ARTHUR J. LOGAN, HAWAII ADJUTANT GENERAL, STATE OF HAWAII

General LOGAN. Chairman Wicker, Ranking Member Schatz, all the Members of the Senate committee, thank you very much for the opportunity to be here today. I'm Major General Arthur Logan. I'm the Adjutant General for the State of Hawaii, and the Governor appointed me as the State's single point of contact for FirstNet in January 2015. And when he first called me the "SPOC," I had to think back to Star Trek in 1970s and I had to touch the top of my ears to make sure they weren't pointed. But I gather they're rounded, so everything was good.

[Laughter.]

General LOGAN. But I'm also the Director of Emergency Management and I'm the Homeland Security Adviser to the Governor. And if that's not enough, I also oversee the Hawaii Army and Air National Guard. From those perspectives and my 20 years of law enforcement experience, I want to share with the Members of this committee the importance of FirstNet.

At the time I was appointed in January 2015, the team had already been engaged in Hawaii in preparing for the deployment of FirstNet. Much of the effort focused on education and outreach to public safety and public policy stakeholders as well as working toward establishing governance, a Governor's model, and strengthening Hawaii's current public safety communications infrastructure.

My first year and a half on the job involved briefings from key staff in Hawaii, meeting with FirstNet leadership, and attendance to the biannual FirstNet SPOC meetings and leading State efforts to develop key public safety communications plans. So let me just cover a few of the brief activities.

Hawaii sponsored the first FirstNet forum for non-contiguous states and territories in July 2014. So Hawaii had the foresight to anticipate the needs and concerns of non-contiguous states, such as Hawaii, Alaska, Guam, American Samoa, the Commonwealth of the Northern Mariana Islands, Puerto Rico, and Virgin Islands. And we know we're different than our sister states of the Lower 48, who are connected by borders and could share coverage.

To that end, in 2014, Hawaii sponsored the first ever non-contiguous states and territories meeting on the island of Kauai. The attendees included policymakers in government and public safety and communication subject matter experts from Hawaii and Alaska and the territories from the Virgin Islands, Puerto Rico, Guam, and American Samoa.

FirstNet's leadership and the leadership of the Department of Homeland Security, Office of Emergency Communications, walked participants through the evolution of technologies used in public safety communications, from the current standard of land mobile radios to the future of public safety broadband. FirstNet heard directly from these jurisdictions and actively participated in our dialog.

A year later, in July 2015, Governor Ige and I sponsored executive level FirstNet briefings. We invited the CEO, T.J. Kennedy, and the Director of Government Affairs, Ed Parkinson, who flew to Hawaii and engaged in the Governor's Cabinet to bring the new leaders up to date on the concept of FirstNet and how it may add value to public safety in Hawaii.

And then in August 2015 was our FirstNet State consultation. FirstNet brought its technical and state plan staff to Hawaii for a day and a half meetings with all Hawaii stakeholders. While FirstNet updated the attendees on the progress of the project, Hawaii stakeholders of over 90 county, State, and Federal partners also had the opportunity to inform FirstNet directly about the challenges in public safety and communications that arise in Hawaii.

Over the time of the meeting, there was an active participation by the community, and good questions were generated. It was said that it's the first meeting I've been to in Hawaii where people stayed the whole time, they were not out on the beach enjoying the fine weather.

Later on, the FirstNet environmental team came out to Hawaii and proposed a problematic environment impact statement, held public meetings on Oahu, and shared their findings to the public.

And, last, data submissions. We've worked within our state, county, public safety, and community throughout Hawaii to supply FirstNet with a great deal of data regarding specific communications needs for public safety throughout the State, and FirstNet will use that data in putting together our state plan.

So in conclusion, as the State's single point of contact, I'm grateful to the Committee for the opportunity to share Hawaii's perspectives and look forward to any questions.

Thank you.

[The prepared statement of General Logan follows:]

PREPARED STATEMENT OF MAJOR GENERAL ARTHUR J. LOGAN,
HAWAII ADJUTANT GENERAL, STATE OF HAWAII

Chairman Wicker and Ranking Member Schatz, and all Members of the Senate Commerce Committee subcommittee on Communications, Technology, Innovation and the Internet, I would like to thank you for the opportunity to appear before this subcommittee to provide the perspective of the State of Hawaii with regard to the progress of FirstNet.

I am Major General Arthur J. Logan, Adjutant General for the State of Hawaii. Governor Ige appointed me as the State Point of Contact (SPOC) for FirstNet, a designation I have held since January 2015. I am also the Director of Emergency Management, and the Homeland Security Advisor to the Governor, and if that isn't enough, I also oversee the Hawaii Army and Air National Guard. From those perspectives, and my twenty years of Law Enforcement experience, I want share with members of this committee the importance of a Nationwide Public Safety Broadband Network (NPSBN), also referred to as FirstNet.

Background: At the time I was appointed Adjutant General in January 2015, Hawaii's team was already engaged in preparing for the potential deployment of FirstNet in Hawaii. Much of that effort was focused on education and outreach to public safety and public policy stakeholders, as well as working toward establishing a governance model to strengthen Hawaii's current public safety communications infrastructure. My first year and one-half on the job involved briefings from key staff in Hawaii, meetings with FirstNet leadership, attendance at the bi-annual FirstNet SPOC meetings and leading state efforts to develop key public safety communications plans.

Provided below is a brief summary of activities in Hawaii to engage stakeholders:

1. *Hawaii Sponsored FirstNet Forum for Non-Contiguous States and Territories in July 2014.* Hawaii had the foresight to anticipate that the needs and concerns of the non-contiguous states (HI and AK) and territories (GU, AS, CNMI, PR, and VI) were different than those of sister states on the mainland. To that end, in 2014, Hawaii sponsored the first ever meeting of the non-contiguous states and territories in the county of Kaua'i: "Bodies of Water/Bodies of Land: The NPSBN Challenge". Attendees included policy makers in government and public safety and communications subject matter experts from Hawaii and Alaska and from the territories of the U.S. Virgin Islands, Puerto Rico, Guam, American Samoa, and the Commonwealth of the Northern Marianna Islands. FirstNet leadership and leadership of the Department of Homeland Security Office of Emergency Communications (DHS/OEC) walked participants through the evolution of technologies used in public safety communications, from the current standard of land mobile radios to the future of public safety broadband. FirstNet heard directly from these jurisdictions and actively participated in dialogue with leadership as to the challenges.

2. *Governor Ige Sponsored an Executive level FirstNet briefing to his new cabinet appointees in July 2015.* As the newly elected Governor, Governor Ige felt it important to have key cabinet directors understand FirstNet and its importance to public safety. FirstNet CEO TJ Kennedy and the Director of Government Affairs, Ed Parkinson, flew to Hawaii and made a presentation to the Cabinet to help bring these new leaders up to date on the concept of FirstNet, and how it may add value to public safety in Hawaii.

3. *FirstNet State Consultation Meeting, August 2015.* FirstNet brought its technical and state plan staff to Hawaii for the day and one-half meeting with Hawaii stakeholders. While FirstNet updated the attendees as to the progress of the project, Hawaii stakeholders (over 90 from the counties, state agencies, Federal partners), also had the opportunity to inform FirstNet directly about the challenges in public safety communications that arise in Hawaii. Over the time of the meeting, there was active participation by the community and good questions were generated. It was said that "it's the first meeting I've been to in Hawaii where people stayed for the whole time!"

4. *Programmatic Environmental Impact Statement (PEIS)*. The FirstNet Environmental team prepared a PEIS report and held a public meeting in Oʻahu to share findings with the public. The Report was sent for public comment as well.

5. *Data submissions*. We have worked with our state and county public safety community throughout Hawaii to supply FirstNet with a great deal of data regarding the specific communications needs of public safety throughout the State. FirstNet will use this data in putting together the State Plan for Hawaii.

Opportunities Created

Governance: Good governance means support of innovation. As we stand up strong governance for our current environment, the foundation is laid for governance of FirstNet in Hawaii. Hawaii formed the Statewide Interoperable Communications Executive Board (SIEB); the focus of which is specifically public safety interoperable communications. We look to build upon its charter to include planning for FirstNet and considering Cyber challenges.

Focus on Public Safety Communications: Hawaii is focusing now, more than ever, on public safety communications. FirstNet precipitated that discussion.

National Governors Association (NGA) Policy Academy on Public Safety Interoperable Communications: As one of five states selected to participate in the NGA Policy Academy, sponsored in collaboration with DHS/OEC, the Governor tasked me to further develop a Governance entity that will drive the success of our public safety communications operations, both in our current environment of land mobile radios and into the future with FirstNet/public safety broadband.

Federal Communications Commission (FCC): Working on FirstNet has opened the door to opportunities to better understand the role of this regulatory body in all aspects of our communications environment.

State E911 Board: My office is forging a collaborative relationship with the State E911 Board to look at synergies among stakeholders.

Statewide Communications Interoperability Plan (SCIP) and SCIP meetings: Stakeholder driven meetings to discuss, in the context of the big picture of homeland security, how our communications system(s) are working, where are the gaps, what are the strengths—all of these are elements of planning for FirstNet.

The Governor and State role in FirstNet

These and similar efforts around the country assist FirstNet in the development of State Plans. Once an individual state plan is developed by FirstNet and presented to a state, the governor has the critical role of accepting the FirstNet plan for network coverage within the state—known as "opt-in"—or deciding to seek approval and funding for construction of an alternative radio access network (RAN)—known as "opt-out."

Opt-in/opt-out: There is no decision nor a basis for the decision at this time. Hawaii will work with FirstNet in the development of the State plan as long as the dollars are available to support staff. The State intends to continue collaborating with other states now issuing requests for information; we believe such information will help Hawaii develop its own business plan and more fully inform our review of a proposed state plan.

Funding: There is not enough money available to perform due diligence on the Hawaii State Plan that will be provided by FirstNet. Hawaii's Federal grant dollars for FirstNet will likely be exhausted before receipt of the draft state plan expected in the first or second quarter of 2017. The Federal formula for allocating money to the states consistently understates the cost of travel for stakeholders in Hawaii where counties are separated by water, the cost to attend meetings on the mainland is exorbitant, and there is a lack of full time resources to perform the type of work needed to prepare an informed recommendation to the Governor with regard to a decision to "opt-in" or "opt-out." We want to ensure that the Plan provides the necessary coverage in all areas of the state, including rural and high risk areas, such as tourist locations and port facilities. Thus, Hawaii believes FirstNet should make available additional funding for the state so we can properly evaluate our state plan before its presentation to the governor for a decision. Such funding will allow for a truly collaborative effort in the design of the state plan to best serve our public safety stakeholders.

Issues Specific to Hawaii

Relevant Information Meetings are not held in Hawaii: Hawaii is a remote and beautiful archipelago in the middle of the Pacific Ocean with its some 1.2 million inhabitants. Holding relevant national meetings in the state, which would help educate our constituents, is frowned upon. It is often said: "we can't meet there; it's the optics." On the other side, there is inadequate funding to send our stakeholders to the types of meetings that will help increase their skills and knowledge. This may present a challenge to deployment of FirstNet.

Geographical Diversity. Hawaii has urged FirstNet to consider the isolated nature, diverse geography and unique characteristics of the State in designing a solution to meet the public safety broadband requirements. Hawaii is the most isolated population center on the face of the earth with almost 2,400 hundred miles of ocean separating Hawaii from the west coast of the continental United States.

The Hawaiian Archipelago consists of scattered points of land stretching over 1,600 miles, making communications extremely important and difficult. As a chain of islands, Hawaii does not have an adjoining state to share support and coverage.

Hawaii has four counties that encompass the eight named islands. The State Capital and largest city is Honolulu, located on the island of Oahu. The consolidated City and County of Honolulu includes an urban area on Oahu with a population of approximately one million. Although Honolulu is a densely populated urban center, there are many rural areas of low population throughout the State. Such areas have critical public safety needs that require the same access to FirstNet.

Tourism: Tourist population impacts state services. Each day, on average, the State entertains some 300,000 tourists from all over the world. Many enjoy the natural beauty of Hawaii by visiting beaches, mountains, hiking trails and remote areas throughout the state. Accidents, medical incidents, and other public safety emergencies involving tourists are inevitable and must be dealt with effectively by public safety responders.

Military: Hawaii also houses approximately 70,000 military personnel from all branches of the Armed Forces stationed at bases throughout the State. Protection of Hawaii's Critical Infrastructure Sectors, including the Hawaii's port facilities is essential as some 80 percent of all Hawaii's goods and commodities flow through our harbors.

Weather: According to the National Oceanic and Atmospheric Administration ("NOAA"), Hawaii is the state at greatest risk from hurricane, tsunami, severe flooding, high surf, and volcanic activity. Many of our inhabitants live in remote areas where communications and response will be extremely difficult.

Hawaii public safety responders include the whole community. In an emergency, first and secondary responders, such as utilities and non-governmental organizations, are a crucial part of the communications community. This is a consideration we will look for in the FirstNet State Plan.

Conclusion

As the State Point of Contact for Hawaii, I am grateful to the Committee for the opportunity to share the Hawaii perspective with regard to FirstNet. We will continue to work toward educating our stakeholders and reinforcing our current public safety communications infrastructure to prepare to be a part of the first Nationwide Public Safety Broadband Network, also known as FirstNet. We are pleased to have a good team in Hawaii dedicated to the best interests of our community.

Senator WICKER. And thank you very much.
And, Mr. Katsaros.

STATEMENT OF ANDREW KATSAROS, PRINCIPAL ASSISTANT INSPECTOR GENERAL FOR AUDIT AND EVALUATION, U.S. DEPARTMENT OF COMMERCE OFFICE OF INSPECTOR GENERAL

Mr. KATSAROS. Good morning, Chairman Wicker, Ranking Member Schatz, and distinguished members of the Subcommittee. Thank you for providing me the opportunity to talk to you today about FirstNet more than 4 years since the passage of the Act that established the authority. I appreciate the invitation to be here to discuss this important topic.

I am the Principal Assistant Inspector General for Audit and Evaluation at the Department of Commerce Office of Inspector General. Our testimony today will focus on three areas that we have identified as ongoing risks that FirstNet will face. We believe that these challenges will become apparent during their efforts to ensure implementation of a nationwide interoperable wireless broadband network for the public safety community. Specifically, these three areas of risk include: one, acquisition management; two, consultations with states and other localities; and three, internal control. Our office believes that if these three areas of short- and long-term risk are not addressed between now and the launch in approximately midyear 2018, the implementation may not succeed.

The first of the three topics I would like to discuss is that FirstNet must effectively manage its acquisitions. The deadline for bidders responding to FirstNet's request for proposal has passed, and they plan to issue a final award as soon as November of this year. The approach to final issuance of this award may prove difficult with everything left to accomplish, and we believe that this schedule is aggressive. We also believe that successfully managing the request for proposal, including evaluating vendor proposals and avoiding conflicts of interest, is critical to the development and implementation of the network, and in executing that implementation, we believe that FirstNet will face geographical challenges in providing service to all 56 states and territories at a competitive cost. Finally, for FirstNet to succeed, multiple Federal agencies will have to collaborate efficiently over the 25-year term of the complex contract.

The second topic I would like to discuss is that effective consultation with states and other localities is critical to FirstNet's success. The Act requires FirstNet to consult with a variety of stakeholders as it builds a network, including, but not limited to, Federal, State, tribal, and local public safety entities. FirstNet has made progress in its discussion and outreach efforts in a variety of ways, to include conducting visits with 55 states and territories, attending conferences, speaking at tribal gatherings, attending national public safety association events and State-hosted outreach meetings, working with law enforcement leaders, and engaging in social media. For the network to succeed, we believe that FirstNet must continue its consultation and outreach efforts to identify public safety needs. While doing this, FirstNet must use input from its consultations to develop individual plans for each State and territory which uniquely satisfy their needs.

And, finally, the third potential risk I would like to discuss is that FirstNet must continue to strength its internal control. In each of our audit reports, we have identified control weaknesses. Similarly, as part of FirstNet's annual financial statement audit, independent auditing firms also identified areas where controls need strengthening. When made aware of these issues, FirstNet management responded appropriately stating their plans to address the areas of concerns and has, in many instances, begun to implement change.

In conclusion, our office feels that these three areas are short- and long-term risks to FirstNet and that the group's efforts to minimize the potential impacts must be both ongoing and attentive.

Chairman Wicker, Ranking Member Schatz, and Members of the Subcommittee, thank you again for this opportunity to appear before you today. I ask that my testimony be entered into the record. And I will be happy to answer your questions.

[The prepared statement of Mr. Katsaros follows:]

PREPARED STATEMENT OF ANDREW KATSAROS, PRINCIPAL ASSISTANT INSPECTOR GENERAL FOR AUDIT AND EVALUATION, U.S. DEPARTMENT OF COMMERCE OFFICE OF INSPECTOR GENERAL

Chairman Wicker, Ranking Member Schatz, and Members of the Subcommittee:

We appreciate the opportunity to testify about the current status of, and challenges encountered by, the First Responder Network Authority (FirstNet). Our testimony today—more than 4 years after the passage of the Middle Class Tax Relief and Job Creation Act of 2012 [1] (the Act) that established FirstNet—will focus on (1) the history of the organization and its work to date; (2) the Office of Inspector General's (OIG's) oversight efforts; and (3) ongoing risks FirstNet faces in their efforts to ensure implementation of a nationwide, interoperable, wireless broadband network for the public safety community.

1. Introduction to FirstNet

Establishment and purpose

Signed into law on February 22, 2012, the Act established FirstNet as an independent authority within the Department of Commerce's National Telecommunications and Information Administration (NTIA). The Act authorized up to $7 billion in funding for the establishment of an interoperable Nationwide Public Safety Broadband Network (NPSBN). The Act also provided $135 million under the State and Local Implementation Grant Program (SLIGP) to promote state outreach, data collection efforts, and planning for the NPSBN.

The Federal Communications Commission (FCC) spectrum auction, completed in January 2015, raised about $45 billion—enough to cover the $7 billion targeted for FirstNet under the Act. FirstNet holds the single Public Safety Wireless Network License for use of the 700 MHz D block spectrum and a pre-existing block of public safety broadband spectrum.

Organization and implementation

FirstNet is governed by a 15-member Board consisting of the Attorney General of the United States, the Secretary of Homeland Security, the Director of the Office of Management and Budget, and 12 nonpermanent members, including representatives from state and local governments, the public safety community, and technical fields. For roughly the first year and a half of its existence, certain FirstNet Board members functioned in management roles. The Board eventually assembled a management team, which assumed all operational responsibilities. As of June 2016, a management team has been assembled to complete FirstNet's mission, including a Chief Executive Officer, President, Chief Counsel, Chief Technology Officer, Chief Information Officer, Chief Administrative Officer, Chief Financial Officer, and Chief Procurement Officer, supported by a cadre of professionals.

So far, implementation of the NPSBN has occurred in the following areas:

- *Establishing an organizational structure.* FirstNet hired key leadership and support staff for its day-to-day operations; developed controls; established its headquarters in Reston, Virginia, and its technical headquarters in Boulder, Colorado; awarded contracts to obtain project management and planning support, professional and subject matter support, and network and business plan development; and signed interagency agreements with other Federal entities to provide key services.

- *Conducting initial consultation and outreach.* FirstNet launched a website, conducted conference calls and webinars with state single points of contact (SPOCs), coordinated with NTIA's SLIGP team, and established its Public Safety Advisory Committee (PSAC).[2] In July 2014, FirstNet began to hold a series of state and U.S. territory consultation meetings. As of May 31, 2016, initial state consultations and data had been received from nearly all the states and U.S. territories. Also, FirstNet has held consultations with tribal nations and Federal users as well as held other discretionary outreach events (speaking en-

---

[1] Middle Class Tax Relief and Job Creation Act of 2012, Pub. L. No. 112–96.

[2] The Middle Class Tax Relief and Job Creation Act of 2012 required FirstNet to establish the PSAC. It was created in February 2013 and consists of 40 members representing all disciplines of public safety as well as state, territorial, tribal, and local governments. See "Public Safety Advisory Committee" at *www.firstnet.gov/about/publicsafety-advisory-committee.*

gagements at conferences, expositions, town hall meetings and summits) in order to educate and engage stakeholders from the public safety community.

- *Implementing a network solution.* In January 2016, FirstNet issued a request for proposals (RFP) for the purpose of seeking a vendor to build and operate the NPSBN. Proposals were due by the end of May 2016. Prior to issuing the RFP, FirstNet sought input from vendors and other stakeholders, issuing multiple requests for information (RFIs), public notices and requests for comment seeking input regarding interpretations of FirstNet's enabling legislation, and a draft RFP. It also has spectrum lease agreements with four public-safety projects funded by grants awarded via NTIA's Broadband Technology Opportunities Program (BTOP) and with the State of Texas/Harris County to provide FirstNet with lessons learned.

FirstNet's expenditures have increased as it has moved toward building the NPSBN. FirstNet reported that it spent less than $250,000 in Fiscal Year (FY) 2012. In FY 2013, it spent about $17 million. In FY 2014, FirstNet incurred operating expenses of $24 million, and $49 million in FY 2015. FirstNet's current focus is on consultation and the acquisition/RFP processes.

2. OIG's FirstNet Oversight

FirstNet's authorizing legislation and subsequent enacted appropriations did not contain an explicit provision for funding permanent, ongoing oversight to prevent and detect waste, fraud, and abuse for FirstNet. In May 2014, OIG entered into a memorandum of understanding (MOU) under the Economy Act with FirstNet to provide specific oversight services that FirstNet sought, such as conducting oversight of FirstNet acquisition processes. Specifically, the FirstNet Chairman of the Board had requested that OIG review ethics and procurement concerns raised by a FirstNet Board member. The agreement was amended in November 2014, providing additional funds and extending the MOU through September 30, 2016. On May 27, 2016, FirstNet moved to terminate the MOU, which we are now closing out over a subsequent 90-day period. This will end all FirstNet requests for OIG services. As a result of the cancelling of the MOU, future OIG audits of FirstNet programs and operations will be conducted using OIG's direct appropriation for general oversight—and prioritized along with the Department of Commerce's other 11 bureaus and agencies.[3]

Building on OIG's experience with broadband and public safety programs (for example, the Public Safety Interoperable Communications (PSIC) grant program and BTOP), the team's initial audit and evaluation activities have included:

- tracking the progress of FirstNet by regularly interacting with staff members and covering agency proceedings, as well as monitoring FirstNet and NTIA for key actions taken to implement the network;
- developing an initial risk assessment in FY 2013 and routinely reassessing risk as part of annual Department-wide assessments;
- identifying FirstNet as a management challenge in our FYs 2013–2016 *Top Management Challenges* reports, noting challenges related to procurement, internal control, staffing, and stakeholder consultation; and
- providing an information memorandum for FirstNet in February 2014 to identify FirstNet's initial management challenges, including establishing an effective organization, fostering cooperation among various state and local public safety agencies, integrating existing grants to enhance public communications capabilities into FirstNet, and creating a nationwide long-term evolution network.

In December, 2014, we issued our first audit of FirstNet.[4] Our findings addressed financial disclosure, the monitoring of potential conflicts of interest, contracting practices, and oversight of hiring. We made nine recommendations. In our opinion, FirstNet took the findings seriously and has made progress towards implementing our recommendations. Subsequent audits covered FirstNet's hiring challenges, need for comprehensive planning and monitoring, and inconsistent implementation of

---

[3] Commerce agencies and bureaus are made up of the Bureau of Industry and Security, Economic and Statistics Administration (includes the Bureau of Economic Analysis and U.S. Census Bureau), Economic Development Administration, International Trade Administration, Minority Business Development Agency, National Institute of Standards and Technology, National Technical Information Service, National Oceanic and Atmospheric Administration, U.S. Patent and Trademark Office, and NTIA.

[4] *FirstNet Must Strengthen Management of Financial Disclosures and Monitoring of Contracts* (OIG–15–013–A), December 5, 2014.

controls,[5] and identified opportunities to improve the effectiveness of the Federal consultation program, including strengthening accountability, and increasing Federal input.[6]

In March 2015, we submitted written testimony to the United States Senate Committee on Commerce, Science, and Transportation, which contained information regarding FirstNet's implementation of the NPSBN, the establishment of an OIG audit team dedicated to FirstNet oversight, and continuing challenges facing the program.[7]

In January 2016, we initiated an audit of FirstNet's management of interagency agreements, which provide important services such as human resources, financial management, and procurement and accounted for approximately 30 percent of incurred FY 2015 expenses. Finally, we have also prepared a risk-based analysis of potential future audit areas.

3. Ongoing Risks Facing FirstNet

More than 4 years since the passage of the Act, FirstNet faces a wide range of short and long-term risks.

A. FirstNet Must Effectively Manage its Acquisitions

FirstNet's award schedule is aggressive. The May 31, 2016, deadline for bidders responding to FirstNet's RFP has passed. FirstNet intends to make a final award as soon as November 2016. To meet a November goal, FirstNet must now have an approach to evaluate proposals received, including identifying qualified personnel to evaluate the proposals and ensuring that these personnel do not have conflicts of interest.

The successful bid must meet the goals established by the RFP. FirstNet adopted an objectives-based approach in its RFP—rather than a traditional requirements-driven model—to provide industry the maximum opportunity and flexibility in the development of innovative solutions for the NPSBN. According to FirstNet, providing this flexibility enables offerors to illustrate their intent in their proposals to meet or exceed the high-level objectives illustrated within the RFP.

As the RFP points out, FirstNet must provide services at competitive prices given constrained local, state, and Federal budgets. It must also be self-sustaining. FirstNet must leverage existing infrastructure, obtain optimal value for excess network capacity, and optimize its pricing structure in order to deliver a high-quality, affordable broadband network and services to the Nation's first responders. In addition, local emergency communications needs are typically met by separate networks using different technologies, and each jurisdiction has its own laws and procedures for building, managing, and funding communications infrastructure. Among the challenges facing FirstNet is accommodating current emergency response systems of localities and their future needs without compromising the benefits of a national network. FirstNet officials have stated that the evaluation process will also include negotiations with potential contractors. Successfully managing the RFP—evaluating vendor proposals and avoiding conflicts of interest—is critical to the development and implementation of the NPSBN.

FirstNet is a nationwide network with geographical challenges. FirstNet has identified what it refers to as "the coverage challenge." That is, the geography of the 56 jurisdictions is varied, with the bulk of the population residing in about 5 percent of the U.S. land mass. The rest of the population resides in rural and wilderness settings. The 3.8 million square miles to be covered by the network will include urban, suburban, rural, and wilderness areas, as well as islands. FirstNet must offer public safety grade services at a cost that is competitive to all users and pay particular attention to coverage of rural areas, a subject specifically prioritized by the Act.

Multiple Federal Government stakeholders must effectively coordinate. The contract is complex and has a 25 year term. The RFP was issued by the Department of the Interior on behalf of FirstNet. For FirstNet to succeed, all parties at Commerce and Interior must collaborate harmoniously and efficiently over the course of a lengthy contract term.

---

[5] *Audit of FirstNet's Workforce and Recruiting Challenges, Participation at Discretionary Outreach Events, and Internal Control* (OIG–15–036–A), August 14, 2015.
[6] *Audit of FirstNet's Efforts to Include Federal Agencies in its NPSBN* (OIG–16–017–A), February 8, 2016.
[7] *First Responder Network Authority's Progress and Challenges in Establishing a Public Safety Broadband Network* (OIG–15–019–T), March 11, 2015.

B. Effective Consultation with States and Localities is Critical to FirstNet's Success

FirstNet must continue its consultation efforts to identify public safety needs for the NPSBN. The Act requires FirstNet to consult with a variety of stakeholders as it builds the network, including, but not limited to, federal, state, tribal, and local public safety entities. The Act also requires FirstNet to consult with SPOCs from each state and territory, and the Act authorizes the SLIGP, which provides resources to those states and territories to consult with FirstNet and plan for the NPSBN. NTIA administers SLIGP and awarded grants totaling $116.56 million.[8] FirstNet must incorporate consultation input into an effective network design that meets public safety needs.

FirstNet must use input from consultation in order to develop individual State Plans for each state and territory. After the completion of the RFP award process, a key next step is for FirstNet to deliver these State Plans to each governor regarding FirstNet's plan to deploy the Radio Access Network (RAN) within the state or territory.[9] Each governor will decide whether it will opt-in to the delivered plan (that is, FirstNet takes on the responsibility of building the RAN) or opt-out (the state or territory takes on the responsibility to deploy, operate, and maintain the RAN within its jurisdiction.) Effective consultation and outreach will increase the likelihood that FirstNet (1) develops State Plans that meet the unique needs of the state or territory; (2) designs a nationwide network that receives adoption and support from the public safety community nationwide; and (3) provides effective guidance to opt-out states regarding RAN design and NPSBN requirements.

FirstNet has made progress in its consultation efforts. FirstNet established a state consultation process, completed initial consultation visits with 55 states and territories, and has begun to hold follow-up meetings. FirstNet received data from 54 states and territories to better understand their network public safety needs, including data on (1) network coverage, (2) users and operational areas, (3) network capacity, and (4) current services and procurement. FirstNet conducted outreach to the public safety community by, for example, attending conferences, speaking at tribal gatherings, attending national public safety association events and state-hosted outreach meetings, working with law enforcement leaders, and engaging social media. FirstNet also established a Federal consultation process to seek input from Federal agencies and departments across the country.

C. FirstNet Must Continue to Strengthen Its Internal Control

As FirstNet's administrative processes have evolved to meet continuing challenges, it has needed to balance expediency and accountability. In order to meet its goals, FirstNet has grown rapidly—Federal employees and contractors increased from 123 to 198 in FY 2015.[10] And adding to its many challenges, FirstNet is limited by the Act to a maximum of $100 million for administrative costs over a 10 year period.

The Government Accountability Office (GAO) has defined internal control as ". . .a process effected by the entity's oversight body, management, and other personnel that provides reasonable assurance that the objectives of the entity will be achieved. . .."[11] GAO recognizes that internal control procedures can be operational-, reporting-, or compliance-based.

OIG and independent audit firms have identified areas for improvement. FirstNet continues to implement and strengthen internal control throughout the organization; however, opportunities for improvement remain. In each of our FirstNet audit reports, OIG has identified areas needing improvement, specifically in regards to processes and controls. These reports have resulted in numerous recommendations for improvement across FirstNet and the Department of Commerce. Similarly, independent auditing firms, as part of FirstNet's required yearly audit,[12] have identified areas where FirstNet controls needed strengthening. The Independent Auditor's report for FY 2014 and 2015 noted that Commerce's annual financial statement audit included findings regarding information system access and configuration management, which the auditor noted as a FirstNet significant deficiency due to its reliance on Commerce information systems. It recommended that FirstNet develop a general ledger transaction review processes to compensate for the deficiency. In all in-

---

[8] The State of Mississippi did not receive SLIGP funds.

[9] FirstNet has estimated it will complete draft state plans around May 2017 and will finalize and deliver state plans by the end of 2017.

[10] FirstNet, February 2016. *FY 2015: Annual Report to Congress,* p. 7.

[11] GAO, September 2014. *Standards for Internal Control in the Federal Government,* GAO–14–704G, OV1.01, p. 5.

[12] *See* 47 U.S.C. § 1429.

stances, FirstNet management responded appropriately, stating their plans to address the issues.

FirstNet has, in many instances, begun to implement changes to its process prior to issuance of the reports, and OIG has reviewed and accepted FirstNet's action plans addressing all report findings.

FirstNet has taken steps to improve internal control. At the March 16, 2016, meeting of the Board, FirstNet's Chief Financial Officer reported the actions FirstNet has taken to improve its internal control process included:

- Adoption of an Internal Control Implementation Plan
- Completion of its first risk assessment
- Enhancement of FirstNet's financial management procedures
- Development of a Core Assessment Team to evaluate internal controls

FirstNet faces additional award challenges. For example, FirstNet must prudently manage the Band 14 Incumbent Spectrum Relocation Grant Program, established to clear spectrum for the NPSBN. FirstNet has begun the process for awarding grant funds to public safety entities. In addition, as a fairly new organization requiring extensive travel and small purchases, travel and procurement card expenditures pose a risk.

FirstNet has noted several upcoming milestones for the deployment of the NPSBN. See figure 1. As FirstNet moves towards these next phases of implementing the NPSBN, continued improvement and oversight of FirstNet's processes will be critical.

Figure 1. Notable Milestones for the **NPSBN**

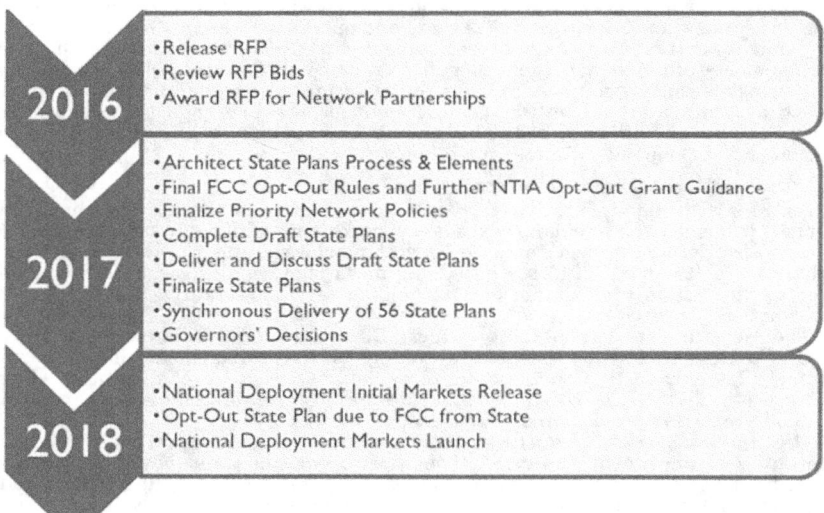

Source: FirstNet, March 2016 Board Meeting

We will continue to keep the Committee informed of FirstNet's progress with respect to the challenges discussed here—and any others we identify through our audits and investigations.

I will be pleased to take your questions.

Senator WICKER. Well, thank you very, very much. And let's do 5-minute rounds of questioning.

Mr. Poth, let's talk about the fact that $7 billion doesn't go as far as it used to go. The $7 billion really was startup fundings not intended to sustain the network for very long. With vastly rural populations having differing emergency needs, what challenges do you have there, and what are your thoughts about covering the rural areas of this Nation? And also with regard to that, once FirstNet is deployed, it's going to charge user fees. Do you think the user fees will generate enough revenue to sustain FirstNet? And is this going to be a problem for rural areas in terms of a cost burden?

Mr. POTH. Thank you very much for the question. And you're exactly right, Senator Wicker, $7 billion doesn't go as far as it used to.

So what we have done with the $7 billion, but more importantly, the 20 megahertz of spectrum that Congress gave FirstNet, that becomes the true value prop to then sit at the table with a partner to come together with their assets and our assets, and we believe the 20 megahertz of spectrum is beachfront property, and we should and will maximize the value of that for public safety. We expect that the commercial partners will come with X amount of capital on their side to start the nationwide buildout of the broadband network.

Part of the components that we've built into the RFP also we are not satisfied just to attack the densely populated areas, we are also very focused on the rural coverage. And even though it's a statutory requirement, we've built into the RFP that every phase of the buildout, at least a rural coverage component, will be contained in there.

We expect our commercial partners, who are typically incentivized, by only going out as far as economically feasible, we'll have to look at that mandate, and we're expecting, through the responses, exactly what the coverage components can be.

We've also required in the RFP with each phase of the build-out rural coverage components with by the fifth year of the build-out, 100 percent of what they have proposed in rural coverage will be accomplished.

We've also, to address concerns about cost out in the rural areas, we are driving in through the RFP, and with our partner for public safety, preferred pricing, and we expect the commercial partner to be very successful, and we hope that they are, in commoditizing the excess spectrum on the commercial side that will keep the fees and the revenues coming into FirstNet for not only the sustainability but also keep the costs down for public safety users, whether they're in rural, urban, or suburban areas.

So we think with all those various factors together, we have provided a platform for success for both the public safety and the partner to be successful on this contract.

Senator WICKER. OK. Well, continue to keep us posted on that.

You know, in the 1 minute 42 seconds remaining, I don't know if I can ask you to respond to Mr. Katsoros's testimony, but he did mention some concerns, no doubt about it, particularly about FirstNet continuing to strengthen its internal control, and I think the clear message is that it's not where it needs to be. That's the way I took the testimony.

So let me ask you, what—your team has participated in outreach efforts throughout the country to assess the needs of each State. What do you—do you believe the decisionmaking process, as it stands today, is as good as it should be?

Mr. POTH. There is obviously room for improvement in anything that you do, but I'll make a run at trying to answer some of the concerns. So on the acquisition management, we have a very rigorous process in place to ensure that the ultimate evaluation——

Senator WICKER. Well, let me just—let's go then to the one that I specifically mentioned——

Mr. POTH. OK.

Senator WICKER.—which FirstNet must continue to strengthen its internal control. And I do believe I've characterized the testimony as that it's not where it should be.

Mr. POTH. Right. I think we believe that the internal controls that have been in place, and thanks to the work of working collaboratively with the Inspector General, we've instituted even more rigor in the internal controls and audits, both within FirstNet with compliance committee reviews, people, and processes, we've strengthened those, and with the Inspector General's audits, I think we believe now that the controls that are in place are allowing us to be successful for the future, for the partnership going forward.

Senator WICKER. And do you think the decisionmaking process, as it stands today, is as good as it should be?

Mr. POTH. I believe so. I have a very strong team that I'm extremely proud of, and I'm buffered by a Board of Directors that the statute is enabled that takes expertise from both the Federal Government, from the wireless community, and financial communities, and when you bring those two together, I think the decisionmaking process is solid. Obviously, as we are forging new territory, there may be twists and turns, but I am fully confident with the team that is in place, we'll be able to navigate those turns.

Senator WICKER. Thank you very much.

Senator Schatz.

Senator SCHATZ. Thank you, Mr. Chairman.

My first question is for Mr. Poth. Mr. McLeod, from NGA, talked about sort of a "choice of words" question with respect to whether or not states and Governors and single points of contacts are constituents or partners. And as a former Lieutenant Governor and a former member of the State administration, I'm kind of sensitive to that on behalf of State governments. And I would just like your assurance that you're listening to Mr. McLeod, and by virtue of listening to Mr. McLeod, hearing that concern, and that we have your commitment working on a going-forward basis with the State administrations and TAGs and others that we really are going to be in a partnership situation rather than sort of a grantee/grantor relationship.

Mr. POTH. No, absolutely. The states and the people that are leading those efforts in the States for public safety and for FirstNet are a critical component. They are truly the tip of the spear of what we're trying to enable, and the partnership is very, very important to us. We spend a lot of time trying to overcommunicate to the States. We don't view them as constituents, but they are critical partners, just like public safety and just like our Federal partners.

Senator SCHATZ. Thank you. And to General Logan, and this is to the question of opting in versus opting out. What Mr. McLeod said was essentially that under the statute, opting out is a mirage.

I don't know if that's an overstatement or not, but that's the gist of it, it is very tough to opt out. So I want to actually focus on opting in. I understand you went through a pretty good process with Governor Ige and your team. And I would like you to kind of explain how you came to opting in and how much support you thought you got from FirstNet in that process.

General LOGAN. Senator, thank you very much for the question. I would say, going back to one of your—the earlier question, when FirstNet came out to brief the Governor's Cabinet, I kind of got with the team beforehand and I sat down and gave some of the interesting nuances of localism and how we, in Hawaii, perceive people that come from D.C. into our state, and I asked them not to wear a suit and tie, I asked them to come in an Aloha shirt when they briefed the Governor, and they did that. And so that kind of warmed over the crowd.

Senator SCHATZ. We appreciate that.

[Laughter.]

General LOGAN. Yes. But also back to this question, I think after they presented to the Cabinet, the Governor and I and Todd Nacapuy, the State CIO, we got together and we kind of went through it pretty quickly, and the Governor's background, I think being a telecommunications engineer and working for telecom companies in the state, I think it was kind of obvious to him that opting in was probably the best solution, although we have not made a final decision. We wanted to wait to see what our state plan is.

Part of the issue the states are having, I think, or at least some of the anxiety the states are having, is we don't know what the RFP is yet, we don't know what the State plan is, so we can only guess at how we can—or what we think is going to happen. So without all the knowledge, it creates some anxiety, so states are somewhat unprepared for what may happen. But I think we're a lot better off than we were with all the communications going on, and FirstNet would be the—they'll—they are an overabundance of communication. If you need something, they will answer your questions. And so they're very receptive to at least—I know in my State they are, and we have a conversation with them.

And so I think, looking at it from the State's IT perspective, what we haven't done yet and what the State CIO and I have discussed a couple weeks ago, was meeting with some of the local vendors within the state, like your Verizons, your AT&T, and just kind of talk through that to see what their perspective is, and maybe we could do it all by ourselves, but I don't think we're there.

Senator SCHATZ. Can you talk a little bit about—I know you've had meetings with other non-contiguous States, but I think some of these concerns that come through the non-contiguous states affiliation also apply to a lot of our rural areas in the continental United States. Can you talk specifically about what the technical needs are and then how you see the kind of revenue distribution and maybe very quickly, General Logan, so I can hear from Mr. Poth as well.

General LOGAN. OK. Well, I have talked to the fellow SPOCs from the other states that are non-contiguous states, and we all have generally the same issue. It's we have, you know, like Oahu is your center of the city and county of Honolulu. That's the major metropolitan area, almost a million people live there. But the neighbor islands, not that many, I think we have 140,000 on the big island, maybe fifty to sixty thousand on the island of Kauai, and close to a hundred on Maui. So how do we—they are generally rural areas, and so how do we guarantee coverage?

One of the things I look at FirstNet is if it's good for the city cop, it's got to be good for the rural cop, firemen, and EMT. So we can't say, well, because you live in the city, you get first priority and we're going to get these guys last. That's not a fair system across the board. So we've got make sure public safety is covered across the board.

Senator SCHATZ. And, Mr. Poth, we have your commitment to work on these issues, not just for non-contiguous states, but for rural areas across the country?

Mr. POTH. Absolutely, and that's a basic premise of our revenue-sharing model.

Senator SCHATZ. Thank you.

Senator WICKER. Thank you.

Senator Gardner.

STATEMENT OF HON. CORY GARDNER,
U.S. SENATOR FROM COLORADO

Senator GARDNER. Thank you, Mr. Chairman. And thank you to the witnesses for your time and testimony today.

Obviously, the potential to revolutionize public safety communications is extremely important. I'm very excited that FirstNet shows Boulder, Colorado, as home of its technical headquarters. It's a great tech community in Colorado, a great tech corridor. Just down the road from FirstNet in Boulder, of course, is the National Institute of Standards and Technology, which is doing great work on public safety communications research at the Communications Technology Laboratory, so we've got a great tech and vibrant economy running in Colorado, and we appreciate you being there.

Mr. McLeod, I want to start with you first. You, in your testimony, talked about FirstNet, "must view states as partners rather than constituents in the consultation process" and mentioned that some states don't believe FirstNet is interested in developing genuine partnerships with the states is how you said it. So following up on a little bit of what Senator Schatz was talking about, could you talk a little bit further about that point and talk about the nature of the meetings that you mentioned and that that nature that have caused the concern in developing those genuine partnerships, that desire to create them, and then talk about the obligation to take that state advice.

Mr. McLeod. Thank you for the question, Senator. So I think— I will say that FirstNet stepped up their efforts over the last year to communicate with states, and as the General said, if there is a question that States have, they've been more than willing to answer those questions. I think my statement reflects the feeling among states that although they may be complying with the letter of the law, that at the end of the day, states don't feel that they are necessarily viewed as full partners.

And maybe just as a quick example, during the development of the State plan, states will be seeing drafts of those plans, but the final plan that will be submitted to them, they will not have an opportunity really to suggest revisions or at least that many revisions would be made. So I think that goes to the sense that were it a true partnership, that states would be more engaged in the development of that plan beyond just the consultations that have been happening.

Senator GARDNER. Please continue if you have anything else.

Mr. MCLEOD. No.

Senator GARDNER. Mr. Poth, do you want to respond to that? And then I can get back to you with an additional question.

Mr. POTH. Sure. Part of the thing that we have to do with the State plans is we're going to be at that point under a contract with our partner. We have submitted into the RFP all the State data unfiltered, what each State and territory felt was important. We're expecting the vendor community now has responded in each particular state how they would go about deploying the network in that state, the random radio access network.

We are then, as Mr. McLeod said, planning on giving a draft to the states so that they have plenty of time to understand the coverage, the cost, and what is being proposed. There are opportunities for feedback, but we are going to have some limitations since it will already be under a contract term as to how much variations, if a state felt it was important, but it is our commitment, as we've always done, to work with the States, and we want to provide that before we turn and have the state plan go final, which then starts the 90-day clock for the Governors because we don't want the states to be surprised at what the plan is with our partner.

But Mr. McLeod is correct. There may be some limitations as to what changes could be done from the draft to the final.

Senator GARDNER. And I think one of the concerns that we have, of course, in Colorado is the geography and the limitations that geography can pose to coverage and the challenges it can pose to that coverage. So are you concerned at all that the approach that you're talking about would—you're not concerned that it would undermine the State consultation process then.

Mr. POTH. No.

Senator GARDNER. And if first it's not relying on that, if you end up with this time crunch that Mr. McLeod is talking about, though, and that you just identified, and you have these unique challenges to geography in the states, who are you looking for, for the expertise then to fill the gap to make sure that you don't have a problem?

Mr. POTH. So if we're in the State of Colorado, for example, all the data and what the State committee felt was important, and public safety, what they felt important, was submitted to the vendors, and it's in the reading room, so they understand what the state's position is and what's important both in the urban and the rural areas, and the Rocky Mountains and those types of areas.

What we're expecting back is how the vendor is proposing to facilitate all of that both with terrestrial and possibly with deployable coverage and what that scenario and the phasing and the build-out would look like for the state. We continue to work with all of the states, and we want to make sure that they understand, you know, the limitations of what may be possible from the contract, although we are absolutely committed to maximize the value for public safety in the states. There will be some limitations probably that we'll expect, but we're going to continue to work with the states.

And the other important thing in the room is we're envisioning—and this will be a 25-year contract—in excess revenues, we are going to reinvest back into the network to where we can advance technology, hopefully expand the rural footprint, so it may not be day one that a state or a public safety agency gets everything they want, but we do have a mechanism in place to continue to fund, not only for our financial sustainability, but to grow the network and with the technology.

Senator GARDNER. Mr. Chairman, can I ask one follow-up question to what he just said?

Senator WICKER. Absolutely.

Senator GARDNER. Thank you. With this revenue issue, and I'm just curious, the prioritization of those funds, network maintenance over network expansion, how will you make that determination?

Mr. POTH. As the excess spectrum funds come in, we're going to be evaluating what's the latest technology. We're building in the contract that we're expecting our partner to evolve and change as the technology without us funding that. That is just part and table stakes for part of this contract. We'll then evaluate what the priorities are with the technological advancements or possibly coverage advancements.

Senator GARDNER. Thank you, Mr. Chairman.

Senator WICKER. Thank you.

We now—we have Daines, Fischer, and then Manchin.

Senator Daines.

STATEMENT OF HON. STEVE DAINES, U.S. SENATOR FROM MONTANA

Senator DAINES. Thank you, Mr. Chairman.

I think in places like Montana technology really removes geography as a constraint. This extends not only to our businesses and our schools, but, of course, to first responders as well. And it's especially important in states like Montana and states like Colorado where we have significant rural areas, first responders can be 50 miles or more away from an accident. So the goal here, I understand, is to provide coverage in 99 percent of the country. As we've seen with mobile wireless coverage, the remaining 1 percent of the country often includes places like Montana.

Mr. Poth, tell me about the future plans, if any, to eventually cover that 1 percent of the country.

Mr. POTH. We hope to—to expect 100 percent coverage is probably a very steep mountain to climb, no pun intended. With the coverage that's required, we're really expecting industry to come back and the technology to evolve to where deployables, satellite technology, and those types of things will enable public safety, especially in remote areas, to still maintain connectivity. The goal of getting to 100 percent coverage throughout the 56 states and territories I think is going to be a pretty aggressive goal.

Senator DAINES. And related to the issue of technology—and I spent a lot of years in the technology business, where it moves at the speed of business versus the speed of government—as you think about the future of where it's headed, how will you keep at FirstNet as it relates to when technology changes? About the time the project is completed, I'm guessing technology will be well ahead of where you end.

Mr. POTH. Right. And that's one of the big focuses and basic tenets of us. As an independent authority, we are going to continue to grow and we are going to continue to push technology. The mention of our labs in Boulder, we are going to be advancing and trying to push public safety innovation and technology for years to grow and with the NIST lab also focused on that, we believe that we are going to be able to optimize the benefits to public safety of what's available.

If you can envision, we don't even know what technology is going to be like in 10 years. I often think—people will say, well, your Android or your iPhones, that was the cutting edge technology, because it is going to go so fast. We're going to have in the contract the ability to grow and push the technology as it goes from 3G, 4G, to 5G, and grow with it, and we're going to have the organization in place to remain the advocates and stewards for public safety with our partner so that they don't lose focus on what's important.

Senator DAINES. We heard today that FirstNet plans to use fees generated from densely populated areas to help fund the build-out in more rural areas. We've had similar funding programs like the Universal Service Fund in place since the 1990s, and we still haven't achieved universal service. How is FirstNet's plan different? And why is your plan going to succeed when others haven't?

Mr. POTH. We have a pretty focused mandate and mission, it's to serve public safety regardless of jurisdiction, regardless of state, and so that's one of our driving forces. The other thing that we are going to do is we are going to remain responsible and accountable to public safety. They're not going to let us allow for anything less than that. And our independent board that oversees FirstNet is also going to ensure for years to come that we don't lose focus on what the investments and what the priorities are.

Senator DAINES. As you can imagine, the broadband and the wireless coverage that we do have in Montana is often provided by our rural telecom providers, so I certainly appreciate the requirement that the prime contractor partner with these rural companies. But it's still unclear to me what accountability measures FirstNet has in place to ensure that these partnerships happen with these rural teleco providers.

So maybe you can elaborate what plan FirstNet has in place to ensure that the prime contractors follow through on its commitment to partner with the rural providers.

Mr. POTH. Once we have the bids that are submitted in and evaluated and we get to a contract award, we are going to have specific milestones both on the rural partnership participation and the coverage. Then those milestones become measurable that we are going to enforce, and we try to incentivize through the contract the right behavior, but there are disincentives to ensure that our commercial partner is achieving the coverage and the cost control measures that we've asked for.

Senator DAINES. Now, I understand the selling excess network capacity is key to paying for the network. How will FirstNet ensure that selling its capacity does not end up competing with our existing providers?

Mr. POTH. We believe with the infusion of the new spectrum and the needs of spectrum throughout the country and all different bands, we think that there is going to be sufficient demand on all the spectrums where we don't believe that that will be necessarily a competition or a takeaway for those providers.

Senator DAINES. All right. Thank you, Mr. Poth.

Thank you, Mr. Chairman.

Senator WICKER. You know, it occurs to me when Members come before this committee, they're going to get a lot of questions about rural areas, and it just makes me feel very good about the brilliance of the Founding Fathers. They created a Senate that wasn't totally population based. And it's my pleasure to recognize now the Senator from another rural state, Senator Fischer.

STATEMENT OF HON. DEB FISCHER, U.S. SENATOR FROM NEBRASKA

Senator FISCHER. Thank you, Mr. Chairman. And I won't let you down, I have a couple more questions about rural areas.

[Laughter.]

Senator FISCHER. So, Mr. Poth, I've heard concerns from stakeholders in Nebraska that FirstNet is going to rely heavily on what's referred to as deployable networks in rural areas rather than deploying a fixed network. For example, instead of building a tower in the Nebraska panhandle, perhaps FirstNet is going to bring in a communications vehicle to provide temporary coverage during an emergency.

When we look at tornadoes and fires, all these emergencies that happen in very rural areas, how can we be assured that these deployable networks are really going to be a viable tool for our first responders, and can they move quickly enough to be useful during really these very, very critical times when we have to have a quick response?

Mr. POTH. Right. What we did with the RFP, with it being objectives based, we asked—one of the particular objectives is rural coverage, and we have asked industry, "You tell us what is the best way to solve that requirement." It could be deployables, it could be terrestrial. We don't know how they have come up with the answer yet, but when we get to that point, that could be part of the solution set, but we're asking industry to do what they do best, come up with the most creative solution to solve and that, as previously discussed and pointed out, and hopefully industry has been listening for the last 3 years, rural and rural coverage is a significant component to the success of this network. So we're hoping and very optimistic that there will be some solutions that can address some of those concerns.

Senator FISCHER. And we've also heard some concerns from stakeholders about the deployment of the broadband network that could possibly result in overbuilding, especially of existing commercial networks, and in Nebraska, you and I discussed this previously, that our telecommunications carriers are doing a really

33

good job of bringing service to our rural areas and our underserved areas. Do you have any specific steps that FirstNet is taking to ensure that this overbuilding or what I would consider maybe an inappropriate use of limited funds, might be addressed?

Mr. POTH. We're not expecting nor anticipating an overbuilding, even in the rural areas. If you envision what is happening in technology today, you've heard the term "Internet of Things," and the number of devices that are going to be required to have access to a spectrum, not to mention, obviously, our most important customer, public safety. So we believe as devices and the Internet of things, Internet of public safety things, grows, that the spectrum needs that are currently in use will be saturated. And then also with our—the additional Band 14 that will come into place will just complement that.

Senator FISCHER. OK. Mr. McLeod, have you heard anything from Governors that are concerned about maybe overbuilding existing commercial networks?

Mr. MCLEOD. Thank you for the question, Senator. I think the big concern for Governors is making sure that to the extent possible, using existing resources and infrastructure to build out the network, just to be mindful stewards of taxpayer dollars. I have not heard specifically that that is a big concern for them.

Senator FISCHER. OK. And, Mr. Katsaros, in your written testimony, you list FirstNet's operating expenses for Fiscal Years 2012 through 2015, and you note that while FirstNet spent less than $250,000 in 2012, it spent $17 million in 2013, $24 million in 2014, and $49 million in Fiscal Year 2015. Can you please clarify if all of these numbers reflect spending that would be considered administrative expenses under the Act? And if so, does this upward trend in funding not suggest that FirstNet is going to exceed its allowable authorization for those administrative costs? And what's going to happen in case it does?

Mr. KATSAROS. Thank you for the question. That's an excellent question. Those costs, per our understanding, those are the total costs, so they are not their administrative costs. Their administrative costs are much less than that. They have been trending over the 10-year period at less than $10 million already, so—but there are no concerns on that area at the moment.

Senator FISCHER. So that should be within the $100 million that's been authorized then if that current trend continues for the administrative costs. Is that correct?

Mr. KATSAROS. Correct. They are under—they are well under that.

Senator FISCHER. And, Mr. Poth, do you anticipate that that will happen, that you will be under that $100 million?

Mr. POTH. We will absolutely be under that $100 million.

Senator FISCHER. OK. Thank you very much.

Thank you, Mr. Chair.

Senator WICKER. Thank you, Senator Fischer.

Mr. Katsaros, the 2012 Act established FirstNet as an independent authority within NTIA. Is that, in fact, working out? How is that arrangement working? And what, if any, role does NTIA have?

Mr. KATSAROS. Yes, thank you. That's another good question. We are not aware of another independent authority that is housed within a Federal department other than FirstNet, so when it was created as——

Senator WICKER. It doesn't compute to an IG——

Mr. KATSAROS. Correct. It did not initially. So when we were confronted with an oversight challenge, we were informed that this is an independent authority under NTIA, the National Telecommunications and Information Administration.

So it maintains some of the sort of capacity, administrative capacity, of the NTIA. It allows it to partner with NTIA, allows for us to partner with NTIA, and initially it caused us to sign a Memorandum of Understanding to fund our oversight activity for FirstNet, which we have now canceled, and now we are considering FirstNet under our general appropriation for funding oversight. But the relationship with NTIA exists, and it is part of the law, so we work with both offices.

Senator WICKER. Were you referring to the MOU with Commerce OIG?

Mr. KATSAROS. Correct.

Senator WICKER. OK. Well, OK, now, as I understand it, FirstNet and Commerce OIG agreed to terminate the memorandum of understanding because FirstNet felt that all of the issues had been adequately addressed. Are you satisfied that that in fact is the case?

Mr. KATSAROS. Well, I don't believe that all of the issues would have been adequately addressed. I believe what the cancellation of the MOU was contemplating was that all of the requests for services that were originally considered under the MOU had been addressed. So to the extent that the request, FirstNet's request, for OIG services were included in that MOU, those services have been—we believe those services have been completed. There are many, many more things obviously to do from an oversight perspective of FirstNet that are still to be accomplished.

Senator WICKER. Mr. Poth, would you respond particularly with regard to this independent authority aspect of my question just now?

Mr. POTH. Yes. So while we enjoy certain rights with the independent authority, we do find ourselves from time to time bogged down with some clunky, well-intended Federal processes that do not enable us to remain as quick and nimble and agile as we need to be, you know, for the true public-private partnership. We've had a lot of success sometimes by brute force to work around within the rules.

A lot of times people confuse our need for independence as clouded as that we are trying to not be accountable or responsible, and that's not the case. We have to move very fast. As the Senator earlier mentioned, technology and technology companies are moving very fast, and to be a true private-public partnership, we're going to still need to have more streamlining and more of the constraints that sometimes placed upon an agency within another agency have. So we continue to work with Commerce and with NTIA to streamline those areas, but it is still sometimes constraining.

Senator WICKER. Would it be fair to say that there's a difference of opinion between your shop and NTIA as to what that term actually means, "independent authority"?

Mr. POTH. I don't think there's necessarily a difference of opinion, it's a difference in how it needs to be applied, because NTIA has been a great partner, but they also feel that they are responsible since it is within their organization. So that conflicting wording sometimes creates a little havoc. We've been very successful working in partnership with them, but it does add sometimes additional layers of oversight and checks that sometimes we don't believe necessarily is going to help us get to the value add. We certainly welcome and always will respond to being responsible and accountable for all our actions, but we do look forward to continuing to work with them to streamline it.

Senator WICKER. I don't want to start a fight——

[Laughter.]

Senator WICKER.—but I think you said there was a clunkiness.

Mr. POTH. Yes.

Senator WICKER. I think it would be helpful if you enlightened the Committee about that. What would be an example?

Mr. POTH. Well, there are certain processes. For example, when we submit our annual report to Congress, which is a requirement, and there are up to 10 agencies that this gets circulated and signed off before we can hit the Send button to your offices. We welcome additional recommendations in oversight on certain things and participation, but that introduction of a delay of X amount of time, while it's not fatal, it does push against reports and obligations. If you envision next, as we work in partnership with our private sector partner as we deploy this nationwide network, as certain twists and turns come up with any major effort like this, if we have that same sort of process to make sure that everyone is comfortable with the decision, that clunkiness may result in some certain delays where decisions need to be made, you know, in a more real-time fashion.

Senator WICKER. OK. You know what? I'm going to give you a chance to expand on that answer for the record, and you'll be able to choose your words. But, again, I'm not trying to create strife here.

Mr. McLeod and General Logan, I think I've characterized Mr. Katsaros's testimony as correctly as saying that there are short-comings and that FirstNet needs to step up its game. Would either of you care to respond to the testimony from the IG as to some of the challenges that he has outlined?

General LOGAN. Sir, I'm not sure I really understand the question.

Senator WICKER. OK. Well, let me ask you this, Mr. Katsaros, have I mischaracterized your testimony? It seems that your testimony is that you have some serious doubts about this all coming together as planned and required and as written on paper. Is that correct?

Mr. KATSAROS. I think that's fairly well summarized. I think there are still a lot unknown especially in this pre-award phase. And then with respect to your comments earlier on internal control, in a lot of ways, FirstNet is still a startup organization, and they experienced sort of the typical operational challenges that a startup organization would encounter. And I do appreciate working with FirstNet that they have adjusted and made those changes that were necessary to kind of move them forward so that it's not a distraction, and I think that's the important thing, that these operational challenges and acquisition challenges and procurement issues are not a challenge as they try to do this important work.

Senator WICKER. Are you optimistic that the goals could be met this year?

Mr. KATSAROS. That's a great question, and it's going to be very difficult to answer. Like we keep talking about this pre-award phase in our office, and during this phase, we're looking at a November 1st timeline. We state that that is aggressive. This is going to be—consultations in several phases are going to be ongoing over the next several months, and there are a lot of variables that need to fall in place for this to be successful. So it's a great question.

Senator WICKER. Let us know if the Committee can be helpful. Now, do either of you care to respond to that? If not, we'll——

Mr. McLEOD. Sure.

Senator WICKER. Yes, Mr. McLeod.

Mr. McLEOD. To your original question, I can say that Governors are fully committed to this being successful, and they pushed hard to get the legislation passed in 2012, and they want to see this work and be successful.

I think certainly going forward a big question is just the unknowns. There is—this is—as I said, this is unprecedented in terms of its size, complexity, and scope. So to the extent there are unanswered questions about, for example, Can it be built within existing cost models? What will the user fees be to connect to the network? And are there any long-term administrative and operation costs that States are looking at that maybe aren't anticipated right now?

So I think with just keeping in mind that States want to see it successful, just concerns about just the unknown, and until they get that State plan at the end of this year, States are going to probably hold back and wait to see if they want to opt in or opt out.

Senator WICKER. Thank you very much.

I had a hint that Senators Blumenthal and Klobuchar might be on their way.

Senator Blumenthal.

STATEMENT OF HON. RICHARD BLUMENTHAL, U.S. SENATOR FROM CONNECTICUT

Senator BLUMENTHAL. Thank you, Mr. Chairman, and thank you for enabling us to participate.

Senator WICKER. We learned quite a bit actually.

Senator BLUMENTHAL. So I gathered. Thank you.

[Laughter.]

Senator BLUMENTHAL. And the reason is it's—we have a very distinguished panel, and thank you for having this hearing and thank you all for being here today.

I don't need to tell anybody here that during emergencies, local resources are strained and communities depend on the support of outside organizations in addition to first responders, the United Way, the Red Cross, all kinds of organizations that play a vital role in protecting property and restoring and maintaining the health and safety of individuals. One example, when Connecticut's shoreline was ravaged recently by Superstorm Sandy, disaster relief organizations mobilized quickly, they helped displaced families, they provided them with food and shelter, and the nonprofit United Way of Connecticut supports the state's 2–1–1, a 24/7 Health and Human Services information referral helpline, which plays a critical role in the kinds of emergencies that we encountered in Superstorm Sandy, and other disasters or emergencies. Whether it's snowstorms or hurricanes, floods, clearly there's a need for such organizations to have access to a dependable national public safety broadband network in order to operate as effectively as possible.

But I understand that the states currently lack clarity as to what entities will be able to use FirstNet. I'm concerned about that fact. In fact, according to the statute, all, "public safety entities," shall have access, but it's not clear what that term means, "all public safety entities."

So let me ask you, Mr. Poth, in addition to our first responders, which is law enforcement, fire, EMS, police, what other entities are encompassed in the definition of "public safety entity"? Would it include in Connecticut our United Way, our Red Cross, our community organizations, and the like?

Mr. POTH. Thank you very much for the question. That's a great one. What we've done, and you're correct, the definition is in our statute, and we've leaned upon our Public Safety Advisory Committee led by Chief Chairman Harlin McEwen to help us sort through some of these questions, and as that relates to what's called local control, we've asked them—they represent 40 public safety agencies and associations, international chiefs of police, IFF, international city/county management associations, volunteer firefighters, "What would be, based on public safety's needs, the hierarchy of control?"

So everyone will have access to the network. Where it becomes important is, What is that priority? You mentioned some of the three traditional, police, fire, EMS, and it can also extend to hospitals all the way down to schools and to those volunteers.

So they're helping us work through that as to what is important for local control, and then when we work with our partner, those things will be kind of set up. I think they have up to 19 tiers of priority that they've identified through local control, because you're exactly right, Senator, in a time of crisis, it's not just the first responders that are needed, it is a true community-wide effort that relies on both public and private partnerships volunteers to be an integral part of that response fiber.

Senator BLUMENTHAL. And the structure or fabric of an emergency response also includes hospitals, health care providers, transit authorities, and so forth. They are public safety entities in a sense as well.

Mr. POTH. Oh, absolutely. There are states that have already standing agreements with bus companies if they have to move mass quantities of people out of their area due to flooding and those types of things. That becomes part of the response fabric that you mentioned.

Senator BLUMENTHAL. Let me ask you in the short time I have remaining, at the last hearing on FirstNet, I asked, What can be done to make sure that FirstNet is not hampered by a sluggish hiring process, I don't know whether you recall that question, and that it has the authority needed to hire the best and the brightest most efficiently? And I would like to revisit that question. Have your hiring processes changed or improved?

Mr. POTH. Yes, they have improved, and we like to think that we do have the best and brightest that we've brought to bear. Our technical and our operational and management teams are, I would say, second to none. We do have some of the traditional challenges in the Federal system, but we have developed, working closely with the other agencies and human resources, to streamline that as effective as possible. But we are, you know, competing with a commercial market for some of that talent. We've been very lucky. Because of the mission and the passion our employees have for this mission, that it has become an easier sell.

Senator BLUMENTHAL. Thank you very much. And, again, my thanks to this panel for your contributions to this area of public policy and for your being here today. Thank you very much.

Mr. POTH. Thank you.

Senator WICKER. Thank you, Senator Blumenthal.

Senator Klobuchar.

STATEMENT OF HON. AMY KLOBUCHAR, U.S. SENATOR FROM MINNESOTA

Senator KLOBUCHAR. Well, thank you very much, Mr. Chairman. And thank you to all of you. I'm sorry I wasn't here earlier. We have the Canadians in town, and Senator Crapo and I head up the Inter-Parliamentarian Group. And actually I have a Canada question to cap that off.

But this means a lot to me, this issue. I'm a former prosecutor. Senator Burr and I head up the 9–1–1 Caucus and Next Generation 9–1–1. You know, we've worked hard to update some of our systems and make them more interoperable. This was really called home in my State when we had the I–35W bridge collapse. Despite the fact that there were dozens and dozens of cars in the water when an eight-lane bridge collapsed in the middle of one of the biggest rivers in the country, 13 people died. It could have been so much worse if not for our emergency responders. And I think what doesn't always get a lot of attention was the reason they were able to get people to safety and get them to hospitals so immediately was that the Minneapolis Emergency Community Center—Communications Center received and processed over 500 calls, 51 of which came directly from the scene of the disaster. Seventy-seven men and women were handling those calls, and, of course, no warning whatsoever, not even the warning you would have with a storm, and were able to get those people help. It's an incredible story of work that had been done for years leading into it anticipating some kind of a disaster between our area hospitals.

So my first question would be about interoperability. We had a major shooting of a police officer, and it really changed the way we looked at it because when the police from many jurisdictions were chasing the deranged man who had killed the police officer, they were using 13 different systems, and many of them couldn't communicate with each other. And so that really spurred us on to make some changes. And I know that we've been working on this since 2004.

Mr. Poth, what guarantees can you give the Committee that the feedback gathered from stakeholders in State consultations as States are developing these State plans will be incorporated? And how will FirstNet respond as States continue to gather and provide updated data?

Mr. POTH. Great. Thank you so much for the question. And just those two small examples demonstrated the need and why public safety demanded that this network and that FirstNet deploy this network. What we've done is in the State consultations and the outreach to both the States, to cities and counties and public safety entities, is make sure that they understand the value proposition and the interoperability that is the cornerstone of what we are trying to accomplish with this network. The interoperability even with Canada will be critical because of the border States and those needs and initiatives.

We're expecting that as we continue even post-acquisition and award, to continue the consultation and champion the cause for the States and for public safety with our partner and in the technology world to keep pushing advancements. You mentioned the dependency and interconnectivity with the dispatch centers. The public safety answering points are key components into that first response on a lot of different incidents, and we work closely with APCO and NENA to make sure that their efforts and what's going on with NG9–1–1 is closely tied into what we're trying to accomplish with the broadband network.

Senator KLOBUCHAR. Well, and since you brought up Canada, thank you, so I can report back to our 15 members of the Canadian Parliament who are in town.

[Laughter.]

Senator KLOBUCHAR. Obviously, we're concerned about the level of interoperability since we are right on the Canadian border in Minnesota, as are so many of our States, and you've got the Great Lakes right there, and there's a vast expanse between our two countries. And could you give us an update on the coordination between the two countries and these border areas?

Mr. POTH. Yes. We spend a lot of time with our Canadian counterparts updating them on our progress and what they're doing. We also have the luxury with Canada in that the Band 14 spectrum is the same bandwidth that they also have allocated for their public safety. So although I get outside my comfort level on the technical side, I believe that makes it even more seamless. But we have ongoing exchanges and updates with the Canadian team as they are trying to implement this on their side to ensure timely response for both parties.

Senator KLOBUCHAR. Thank you.

Mr. McLeod, Sheriff Stanek of Hennepin County, our biggest county in our state, serves on the FirstNet board representing law enforcement. And are there some specific needs that firefighters hope to see incorporated into the design of FirstNet? And what do you think can be done to incorporate some of the law enforcement and firefighter concerns?

Mr. McLeod. Thank you for the question, Senator. I think states certainly look to the network as being available to a wide range of first responders, so that would include fire, police. I think that goes back to making sure that there is real value there and that they demonstrate the value to States and to those first responders.

Senator Klobuchar. Thank you.

I just had one last question, and maybe I'll put one more on the record.

But I'll get back to you, Mr. Poth. Newcore Wireless, which is based in Saint Cloud, Minnesota, recently participated in a pilot project with FirstNet in Elk River. The pilot project tested a public safety LTE network in urban and rural areas, and I'm glad that you're looking at those partnerships with rural companies, that's where a lot of our gaps are. I've seen this, and we've got—you know, it's everything from a major case of a fugitive to someone with a snowmobile that broke down in the middle of—and it's a small thing, but it's not a small thing because they are completed isolated and they can't get through even though they have a cell phone.

And it's my hope that FirstNet will not only share the public safety community—serve the public safety community but can also share and spur on these kinds of additional wireless broadband and infrastructure deployment like we've seen in this pilot. Could you talk about this pilot in particular and what you learned from it?

Mr. Poth. The particulars I'm not exactly up to speed on, but I do know that we use that, as we've done with all the early builders, as lessons learned, and we incorporate every one of those events, and we take copious notes to make sure as we work with our new partner, still yet unidentified, to learn from those lessons as we begin the deployment into the Nation. We also are expecting, as you've already noted, through the RFP process, the rural partnerships to be clearly articulated, and the value proposition to go out to the rural areas will be clearly stated in all the State plans.

Senator Klobuchar. All right. Very good. Well, thank you. Thank all of you for your good work.

Mr. Poth. Thank you.

Senator Klobuchar. Sorry I didn't get to everyone, but the Canadians await me. Thank you.

Senator Wicker. Thank you, Senator Klobuchar.

And thank you, gentlemen. I think this has been a very knowledgeable panel and a very enlightening hearing. Thank you very much. And the hearing is closed.

[Whereupon, at 10:51 a.m., the hearing was adjourned.]

APPENDIX

PREPARED STATEMENT OF HON. BILL NELSON, U.S. SENATOR FROM FLORIDA

FirstNet is at a critical juncture. The nationwide network is closer to reality than ever before, and yet much remains to be decided. Just a few weeks ago, FirstNet received responsive bids to its requests for proposal (RFP) for deployment of the network. The carefully crafted RFP, which was the result of extensive preparation and consultation, set forth detailed objectives for the first responder network that any private sector partner has to meet. I know we are all anxious for FirstNet to complete its review of those bids—something it plans to accomplish before the end of this year.

We are not allowed to know the number of bids FirstNet received, nor the specifics of those bids. Indeed, Mr. Poth cannot give us any insight into those bids while we are in this sensitive review period. We all want to know how the private sector responded to the RFP. What do the bids say about how rural areas will be covered? How will FirstNet become self-sustaining? What insights can the bidders provide about how the network will be deployed in states and territories? These are all questions for another day. In fact, one wonders about the timing of today's hearing given the legal and practical constraints on all parties, including FirstNet, who can offer the most insight about network planning and other questions.

Broadly speaking, the legislation creating FirstNet built in a great deal of flexibility in how the network was to be deployed, leaving actual implementation to the private sector partner. The RFP rightly set forth broad objectives to meet the statutory directives, but leaves the details to the private part of what will be the first-of-its-kind, public-private partnership. Selecting a private sector partner likely will not be easy. Will FirstNet's eventual decision make everyone happy? Of course not—that's a given. But is it critical that we get this done? You bet.

When we came together in a bipartisan way more than four years ago to take the important step of creating FirstNet, it was because we knew we needed to give our Nation's first responders—who put their lives on the line each and every day—the tools they need to communicate effectively during emergencies. Governors, mayors, and public safety officials from across the country all joined us to put aside individual parochial concerns and recognize that we all had to work as partners to create a new paradigm if we were to make a truly interoperable network for first responders a reality.

As it's taken several years to get to the RFP stage, that collective will in support of FirstNet may have faded into skepticism in some corners. I fear that some may try to exploit such feelings at the expense of our Nation's first responders. Now is not the time to jump to conclusions or make rash decisions with regard to FirstNet. The process Congress created is working and we will soon know the parameters of the private sector's response to the RFP.

As I have said before, we knew the mission we gave FirstNet would not be easy—but the stakes of inaction were too high. That's why we cannot lose sight of what brought Congress to create FirstNet three years ago—our nation's first responders deserve an advanced nationwide interoperable wireless broadband network to help them do their jobs to protect us all.

———

RESPONSE TO WRITTEN QUESTIONS SUBMITTED BY HON. KELLY AYOTTE TO
MICHAEL POTH

Question 1. Since our last oversight hearing, we have seen increasingly advanced cyberattacks target major companies, government agencies, and critical infrastructure owners and operators around the world. Given these constantly evolving threats, does FirstNet have a plan to ensure its cybersecurity strategy is able to keep pace with new security innovations and technologies in order to remain relevant well into the future?

Answer. Cybersecurity is one of the sixteen key objectives that every offeror of the RFP must demonstrate to meet the requirements of deploying the NPSBN. Included in a cybersecurity solution, an offeror must provide an end-to-end solution for cybersecurity covering everything from devices, to connectivity, physical security to network operations, to applications and other software. The difference with the NPSBN and other networks is that cybersecurity will be considered from the very beginning of the network design, instead of in an ad-hoc or patchwork way. This enables FirstNet and our future partner(s) to consider how to approach threats like malicious attacks in ways before the network is designed.

While there will be no perfect solution to cybersecurity, the benefit of doing this with a private-sector partner is that we can aggregate the lessons, processes, and responses from multiple agencies, companies, and other sources, to become smarter, more proactive, and better informed to protect the FirstNet network. FirstNet intends to leverage expertise from the public and private sector for the benefit of public safety.

The contract term is 25 years, and the RFP requires that the partner show that it has a way to continuously upgrade, maintain, and secure the network throughout the life of the program. FirstNet is still evaluating RFP responses at this time and therefore cannot discuss any specific proposed solutions to the NPSBN. Through the RFP, however, FirstNet has communicated that it fully expects its future partner to have solutions to all cyber threats, including malicious attacks.

Question 2. Additionally, a key challenge to designing cybersecurity into complex systems is doing so without negatively affecting speed and function. Building a national public safety broadband network presents similar challenges. How is FirstNet designing a secure system that also preserves rapid response time and robust functionality?

Answer. FirstNet staff includes those who have served in public safety, from the wireless industry, and, in some cases, both. This has given us the perspective to appreciate the technical challenges and opportunities with deploying the NPSBN, while also focus on meeting the needs of public safety. Through consultation, many States provided us with case studies of how their first responders used data and wireless technologies in everyday activities and during incident responses. This was also extremely beneficial in helping us understand the particulars of each State and geographical challenges that FirstNet will have to meet.

During the New Hampshire initial consultation, the State shared the challenges it faces when responding along its border and throughout its rural and diverse geography. These comments will inform FirstNet's work with its private sector partner(s) to help determine the best possible solution.

We also understand there is a balance between accessibility, speed, and reliability while still achieving security. We have looked at commercial deployments of networks as examples and will be working with our partner(s) to develop a secure network that is usable during incident response. Over time, as we learn from our users about how they have accessed the network, we will continue to work with our partner(s) to improve how the network serves its users.

Question 3. I appreciate FirstNet's diligence to make sure rural areas of the country have access to FirstNet, including the 15 percent geographic requirement for prime contractors to partner with existing rural telecom providers. I have noticed, though, that the 15 percent rural partnership requirement will only be evaluated at a single preliminary stage in the RFP selection process. How will FirstNet ensure that the final accepted contract still includes the rural partnership stipulation? And, once implemented, that the winning bidder follows through on its assurance to partner with rural telecommunications providers for at least 15 percent of the total coverage nationwide?

Answer. Including rural coverage and rural providers are key evaluating factors in the RFP. In the RFP, we ask an offeror to meet 15 percent of its nationwide rural coverage objective with rural providers. When responding to the RFP, an offeror was to provide, on a state-by-state basis, its proposed partnerships with rural providers, and show that on a nationwide-level they met or exceeded the 15 percent minimum target. Fulfilment of this requirement will be monitored throughout deployment and over the lifetime of the contract with FirstNet. The 15 percent rural partnership requirement was a *minimum* threshold in an early stage of the evaluation process. However, that was not the only time that the offerors' rural partnerships will be evaluated. An additional evaluation factor for the RFP is the offerors' rural partnerships over and above the 15 percent minimum threshold as a means of fulfilling the utilization of existing infrastructure, as mandated by Congress, which is one of the sixteen objectives outlined in the RFP.

RESPONSE TO WRITTEN QUESTIONS SUBMITTED BY HON. RON JOHNSON TO MICHAEL POTH

Question 1. Mr. Poth, I have heard that FirstNet is "ahead of schedule and under budget" as it moves to implement the Public Safety Network. Is this true?

Answer. Financial responsibility is one of the key tenants of FirstNet's obligations to deploying a nationwide network. In the Act, FirstNet was given a one-time allocation of up to $7 billion as seed capital and explicit direction that the network and our organization are to be self-sustaining. To be solvent, FirstNet was licensed 20 MHz of spectrum, has the ability to monetize excess spectrum capacity via covered leasing agreements, and can assess certain fees (*e.g.,* for network use or access).

FirstNet has a responsibility to the American people, and public safety in particular, to use these assets wisely. Every day FirstNet does not provide service and maximize the spectrum availability is a day lost to serving public safety and the communities they serve. And for this cause the FirstNet organization is driven to fulfill its mission, which fuels the urgency to deploy this network.

To date, FirstNet has stuck to our announced deadlines, outlined in our publicly available roadmap, and remains within budget. Any delays of the network would be a delay to serving public safety.

Question 2. Mr. Poth, can you commit that FirstNet has no plans to seek additional funds, outside of what has already been authorized, from Congress? Will FirstNet commit to a model that is self-sustaining moving forward?

Answer. FirstNet commits to staying within our budgetary authority and has developed a business plan that we believe will maintain financial sustainability. Being self-sustaining is a factor in driving the speed at which we are executing. We are extremely mindful of our fiscal and legal obligations and do not intend to veer from those responsibilities.

RESPONSE TO WRITTEN QUESTIONS SUBMITTED BY HON. CORY GARDNER TO MICHAEL POTH

Question 1. You indicated in your response to one of my questions at the hearing that FirstNet will send states a draft plan so that they "have plenty of time to understand the coverage, the cost and what is being proposed." And you say further that while there is opportunity for feedback, there will be some limitations since the plan will already be under a contract term, but regardless, FirstNet will work with the states. In light of those comments, do you agree that states should have the ability to alter components of the plan if it will not work for their state?

Answer. FirstNet's mission is to ensure the deployment and operation of a nationwide, interoperable communications system for public safety. This has been demanded by first responders, who desire priority, pre-emption and expanded coverage from what they currently have on existing commercial networks. As FirstNet has limited resources to accomplish this mission, we aim to achieve the best solution for public safety in every state and territory within our financial means. This public-safety focused mission is at the core of FirstNet's consultations with the States and is reflected in the request for proposals (RFP) we issued this year, which seeks a nationwide partner to deploy and operate this system.

FirstNet's goal is to provide the best possible network to meet public safety's needs throughout the Nation. We have been working with our State partners for the better part of two years to understand their unique needs so that the State Plans reflect the desires of each State. FirstNet intends to work with the RFP awardee to tailor the draft State Plans to these State requirements as best we can. Our goal is to produce State Plans that are a product of States' data collection efforts, ongoing consultation activities, and coverage objectives balanced with Congress' mandate for a self-sustaining network. Thus, it is our hope that we can address issues identified by States, without compromising the financial sustainability of the network, through a draft State Plan process in consultation with our State partners.

Question 2. Does FirstNet intend to preempt any state and/or local zoning or other laws in order to implement the network?

Answer. The Act does not contain any express exemption for FirstNet from State and/or local zoning laws. Therefore, FirstNet's commercial partner(s) will be expected to comply with applicable Federal, State, and local zoning laws and their associated regulations. FirstNet will work with States or localities that want to share information on zoning requirements or associated regulations that may impact deployment, operation, and maintenance of the network.

Question 3. Will FirstNet outline the secondary costs to states in the state plan, including for example, the costs to connect a public safety answering point (PSAP) to the network?

Answer. The State Plan will include information on the deployment of the radio access network (RAN) within a State's geographical boundaries. If a Governor chooses to opt-in to the FirstNet State Plan or chooses to take no action at all during the 90-day Governor's decision period, all RAN deployment costs will be borne by FirstNet and not the State.

The State Plan will also outline and describe specific fees and costs that a State *would* bear, if it were to opt-out of FirstNet's State Plan and decide to deploy, operate, and maintain the RAN with State funds. Due to the State having to then develop its own RFP and execute its own procurement to bring on a private sector partner, FirstNet cannot definitively know what the State's costs would be for interconnection and interoperability before a State selects its own partner.

Additionally, the State Plan will include the *optional* costs for public safety entities to subscribe to FirstNet services if the network meets public safety's needs and is determined by the public safety entity to be its best choice for service.

Question 4. I know that there have been public notices and that you have solicited feedback from states and interested parties throughout the drafting process. Is that feedback available to the public? If not, will it be made available? If so, when? If not, why not?

Answer. FirstNet takes transparency of its operational decision-making very seriously, which is why it has frequently chosen to ask for and has received public comments on its actions. The links below are publicly accessible and represent examples of FirstNet's solicited public feedback:

- The Draft RFP documents are all public documents, along with the answers and responses to over six hundred (600) received questions. Those documents may be accessed here: *https://www.fbo.gov/index?s=opportunity&mode=form&tab=core&id=3107e180a6f34e13df3f4fa7f86d55df&_cview=1*

- FirstNet's first public notice and associated comments can be found here: *https://www.federalregister.gov/articles/2014/09/24/2014-22536/first-responder-network-authority-proposed-interpretations-of-parts-of-the-middle-class-tax-relief*

- FirstNet's second public notice and associated comments can be found here: *https://www.regulations.gov/document?D=NTIA-2015-0001-0001*

- FirstNet's third public notice and associated comments can be found here: *https://www.regulations.gov/document?D=NTIA-2015-0002-0001*

- FirstNet's final interpretations and responses to associated comments can be found here: *https://www.federalregister.gov/articles/2015/10/20/2015-26621/first-responder-network-authority-final-interpretations-of-parts-of-the-middle-class-tax-relief-and*

  https://www.federalregister.gov/articles/2015/10/20/2015-26622/final-interpretations-of-parts-of-the-middle-class-tax-relief-and-job-creation-act-of-2012

- FirstNet solicited another round of questions for its final RFP. The associated responses and changes to the RFP made because of the public's immense response (400+ questions) can be found here: *http://www.firstnet.gov/news/firstnet-issues-rfp-nationwide-public-safety-broadband-network*

Question 5. Colorado is a state known for its outdoor recreation and isolated population centers. With these facts in mind, Colorado proposed that 97 percent of the state's area be covered under FirstNet. I cannot blame my state for aiming as high as they possibly could, thinking that FirstNet would propose something slightly lower that they could agree upon. However, FirstNet ultimately proposed coverage of 24 percent of the state's land area. Did FirstNet take into account significant outdoor recreation areas, seasonal population, or isolated population centers when determining its proposed coverage area? Given that Colorado is relatively unique in these respects, do you believe that 24 percent of the state's area is a reasonable coverage goal?

Answer. FirstNet has not proposed any coverage to Colorado or any state at this time. Partner proposed Coverage maps for each state will be available after FirstNet has awarded a contract from its nationwide Request for Proposals (RFP) and draft State Plans have been developed and presented to each State. Current timelines estimate this date to be in calendar year 2017.

In its FirstNet "data collection" submission, the State of Colorado expressed its priorities for timing of the deployment and the need to cover 97 percent of the state geographically. This data, along with other states' data collection efforts, are in the

RFP Reading Room for each of the offerors to review and respond to, focusing on the true needs and priority areas of each State. Because there are costs involved in any network deployment and FirstNet must be a self-sustaining entity, these priority areas were meant to help the offerors' business planning needs so that the States' rural area deployment priorities could be addressed in as near to the order requested by the State as possible (for instance, some States prioritized deployment in their rural State/national parks and recreation areas before other rural locations due to the seasonal visitor spikes that occur in the parks/recreation areas).

The stated "24 percent" coverage cited above was a *starting* point for State to develop their Coverage Objective for the state and the data collection that FirstNet presented to Colorado (and all other States) based on known highways, population centers, and other public safety needs. This Coverage Objectives baseline was then used by States to supplement where they saw additional areas of needed coverage and was not intended as a proposed coverage objective. This information was presented to the bidder community to allow them to properly price the network deployment in their proposals and to identify the cost associated with the states desires.

Question 6. What are the options for a state that opts into the network but then, prior to the expiration of the partnership contract, realizes that it does not meet the state's needs?

Answer. The Act only contemplates a single Governor's decision once presented with the final FirstNet State Plan. However, FirstNet intends to work with States and their local/State public safety entities throughout the 25-year contract, and further throughout the life of the network, to ensure that FirstNet is meeting the needs of public safety. FirstNet had developed a Chief Customer Office (CCO) position to ensure that satisfaction with the deployment by subscribers to the network. It is the FirstNet's goal to ensure that the provider is providing superior service to public safety within each state but staying within the fiscal limitations of sustainably. Even after the network is deployed, there is no mandate for public safety or the States to use the network.

Question 7. What mechanisms will be in place, apart from the financial penalties identified in the RFP, to assure state and local leaders that the public safety network will meet their needs for the next 25 years? How will the operational and oversight models ensure local responders will have a say in the evolvement and review of the network performance (upgrades, expanded coverage & capacity, new features, etc.)?

Answer. State and local public safety users have the ultimate market-driven tool to ensure their needs are being met: the ability to walk away and switch to another service available in the market. FirstNet intends to work directly with State and local public safety entities to meet their needs of expanded coverage and capacity, feature and device upgrades, etc. as they arise. FirstNet and its future partner must listen to and adapt to public safety's evolving situational awareness and operational needs over the next 25+ years to be successful.

Additionally, FirstNet recently announced the creation of a Chief Customer Office (CCO) to prepare for a customer-centric operating environment with a focus of evolving the organization so it is in the best position to work with and serve the public safety marketplace. The CCO includes many of FirstNet's current "User Advocacy" programs, such as Outreach, Consultation, State Plans, and Communications. The office will also encompass future customer service programs, product management, marketing, training, and will continue to evolve to meet FirstNet's public safety customers' needs.

Question 8. Given the difficulty in constructing new sites on Federal land and the lack of existing carrier coverage in much of this area, how will FirstNet achieve significant rural coverage in states with large percentages of Federal land?

Answer. FirstNet appreciates the need for improved connectivity on Federal land across the country and recognizes the difficulty and coordination needed in the construction of new sites. FirstNet will work in close coordination with its Federal, State, Tribal County and local partners to explore deployment opportunities and public infrastructure in these areas. While many solutions will be looked at, in some areas FirstNet may utilize alternative solutions, such as high power equipment (as allowed by the act) deployables and vehicular network solutions to assist in remote areas. FirstNet will be working with States and its RFP awardee to understand the possibilities of deployable coverage in areas with coverage needs that may not be static or as easy to build permanent structures.

Question 9. Are there contingency plans in case the partner is unable to fulfill the obligations required for buildout?

Answer. FirstNet will be fully engaged with our partner to deploy the NPSBN to ensure a timely and effective deployment throughout the lifetime of the contract.

While we will work intently to avoid any missteps in the program, there is always the possibility of project delays or the partner missing buildout targets. This is one of the primary reasons why FirstNet is consulting with States, setting the proper expectations on deployment timelines and coverage, we don't want to over extend our financial position or induce financial risk into the project.

For such contingencies, the Request for Proposals (RFP) outlines a system where FirstNet would intervene and assess the degree to which there may be possible failures to meet deployment targets. Depending on the severity of the missed targets, the partner will be obligated to make disincentive payments back to FirstNet. The disincentive payments are on a sliding scale, and will continue until the program is back on track. If for whatever reason the partner cannot return back to meeting targets in a mutually agreed way, then there is an option for FirstNet to step in and recover the deployment planning.

Question 10. What efforts has FirstNet taken to ensure that its network incorporates strong cybersecurity measures to protect against malicious cyberattacks? How does FirstNet intend to maintain an up-to-date system capable of resisting constantly evolving cyber threats?

Answer. Cybersecurity is one of the sixteen key objectives that every offeror of the RFP must demonstrate to meet the requirements of deploying the NPSBN. Included in a cybersecurity solution, an offeror must provide an end-to-end solution for cybersecurity covering everything from devices, to connectivity, physical security to network operations, to applications and other software. The difference with the NPSBN and other networks is that cybersecurity will be considered from the very beginning of the network design, instead of in an ad-hoc or patchwork way. This enables FirstNet and our future partner(s) to consider how to approach threats like malicious attacks in ways before the network is designed.

While there will be no perfect solution to cybersecurity, the benefit of doing this with a private-sector partner is that we can aggregate the lessons, processes, and responses from multiple agencies, companies, and other sources, to become smarter, more proactive, and better informed to protect the FirstNet network. FirstNet intends to leverage expertise from the public and private sector for the benefit of public safety. A prime example of how we intend to accomplish this is our forth public notice on cybersecurity which was released in October, 2015. The public notice sought solicit input from industry, public safety, and other interested parties as part of our RFP process by asking industry to provide some of the key considerations and concerns with respect to how cyber security should be designed, established, and sustained as the foundation of the NPSBN.

The contract term is 25 years, and the RFP requires that the partner show that it has a way to continuously upgrade, maintain, and secure the network throughout the life of the program. FirstNet is still evaluating RFP responses at this time and therefore cannot discuss any specific proposed solutions to the NPSBN. Through the RFP, however, FirstNet has communicated that it fully expects its future partner(s) to have solutions to all cyber threats, including malicious attacks.

———

RESPONSE TO WRITTEN QUESTION SUBMITTED BY HON. BILL NELSON TO MICHAEL POTH

Question. FirstNet has engaged with numerous public sector stakeholders related to public safety, such as local governments and law enforcement entities. There are also private sector stakeholders in the public safety ecosystem, such as alarm service providers, who are willing to engage with FirstNet on potential use of the network to assist communication with public safety officials and first responders. What is the definition of public safety that FirstNet is using? In addition, how has FirstNet defined the difference between primary and secondary users of the FirstNet network?

Answer. The Middle Class Tax Relief and Job Creation Act of 2012 (Act) defines a "public safety entity" as "an entity that provides public safety services." 47 U.S.C. § 1401(26). In turn, the Act defines "public safety services" as having "(A) the meaning given the term in section 337(f) of the Communications Act of 1934 (47 U.S.C. 337(f)); and (B) includes services provided by emergency response providers, as that term is defined in section 2 of the Homeland Security Act of 2002 (6 U.S.C. 101)." 47 U.S.C. § 1401(27). Thus, under the Act, the definition includes, at minimum, the traditional public safety disciplines (law enforcement, fire, and EMS), as well as any other entities that provide "public safety services."

FirstNet issued public notices providing preliminary guidance and seeking public comment on the "public safety entity" definition, among 63 other key interpretations of the Act that impact operational and economic issues regarding the planning, deployment, operation, and sustainability of Nationwide Public Safety Broadband Network (NPSBN).

[*See* First Responder Network Authority Proposed Interpretations of Parts of the Middle Class Tax Relief and Job Creation Act of 2012, 79 Fed. Reg. 57058 (September 24, 2014); Further Proposed Interpretations of Parts of the Middle Class Tax Relief and Job Creation Act of 2012, 80 Fed. Reg. 25663 (May 5, 2015).] The responses helped inform FirstNet's network planning, including development of our request for proposals (RFP) for the deployment of the NPSBN.

At this time, FirstNet does not plan to announce any final interpretation regarding the definition of "public safety entity" and will rely on the plain-language definition provided by Congress in the Act. However, FirstNet continues to analyze the scope of the definition, the needs of the public safety community, and the likely changing nature of those needs over time in determining whether it is necessary to provide additional guidance.

Pursuant to the Act and FirstNet's Final Interpretations, a "secondary user" is any user that seeks access to or use of the NPSBN *for non-public safety services*. *See* 47 U.S.C. § 1428(a); Final Interpretations of Parts of the Middle Class Tax Relief and Job Creation Act of 2012, 80 Fed. Reg. 63523 (Oct. 20, 2015). Accordingly, while the Act does not use that terminology, public safety entities (as defined by the Act), as a whole, are the "primary" users of the NPSBN.

FirstNet is focusing on developing priority and preemption capabilities so public safety voice, video, and data communications will not be in a figurative "traffic jam" caused by network congestion, which is what happens today in areas or events with a high concentration of users. As part of our work in this area, FirstNet is coordinating with the Public Safety Advisory Committee (PSAC) and the states and territories to help develop a Quality of Service, Priority and Preemption (QPP) framework for the NPSBN. The QPP framework seeks to ensure that the NPSBN remains a "wide open freeway" for public safety, so when public safety traffic increases, the NPSBN should, as quickly and seamlessly as possible, move non-public safety traffic onto other network roadways.

Quality of Service (QoS) is needed to protect access to public safety mission critical services and applications at the required level of quality corresponding to their individual needs. QoS requires assignment of properties such as bandwidth guarantees, usage limits, latency, accuracy, accessibility, and retention.

Priority is the means by which users, applications, traffic streams, or individual packets take precedence over others in establishing a service session or forwarding packets during periods of congestion in the network. Public safety users will require priority access to the NPSBN resources to make their communications (at the required level of QoS) an effective tool in their management of incidents and emergencies.

Lastly, preemption is used together with priority to control use of resources by removing lower priority user active sessions and allowing allocation of resources to higher priority users when network resources are scarce or fully occupied.

For further information on QPP, FirstNet authored a white paper on the subject, which is available in the RFP Reading Room. *See http://www.firstnet.gov/resources/request-reading-room-access.* This paper has served as a reference document, explaining FirstNet's vision regarding QPP, so that potential bidders to FirstNet's RFP were able to develop proposals around these principles.

––––––

RESPONSE TO WRITTEN QUESTION SUBMITTED BY HON. CORY BOOKER TO MICHAEL POTH

Question. New Jersey is using FirstNet spectrum for an exciting public safety broadband project known as "JerseyNet." This project is overseen by Fred Scalera, a recognized expert in emergency communications. The project, which is spread throughout the state and includes areas in the Route 21 corridor between Camden and Atlantic City, explores the use of mobile systems to be deployed in case of an emergency. This project will address a problem that arose during Superstorm Sandy, when storm damage brought down critical telecommunications systems.

This project could be a model for the country, greatly contributing to network functionality in times of crisis. Additionally, because the units are mobile, they can be deployed to assist other states when needed. These mobile units were deployed and successfully used during Pope Francis's visit to Philadelphia last September, and they continue to be tried and tested at large scale events in the region.

What has FirstNet learned from the JerseyNet project? What role does FirstNet envision for the use of deployable assets in a future first responder telecommunications network?

How will you ensure that FirstNet, when deployed, will take advantage of the latest mobile broadband mobile technologies?

Answer. FirstNet acknowledges the contributions of Mr. Scalera and the JerseyNet team. JerseyNet and the other early builder projects that FirstNet supports provide valuable key lessons that have been leveraged in the creation of the FirstNet Request for Proposal. As documented in FirstNet's Fiscal Year (FY) 2014 and FY 2015 Annual Reports to Congress, deployable assets will likely be a key element of the FirstNet network, and FirstNet continues to leverage the collaborative work with the State of New Jersey and NTIA to support planning and implementation of these deployable capabilities. The unique deployable design elements engineered by the JerseyNet team, such as sizing to quickly enable parking garage rooftop deployments, and rack mount assets to provide rooftop deployment flexibility, have been particularly useful. We expect the future network will leverage the important lessons gleaned from the JerseyNet project.

Over the past year, substantial progress was made by the JerseyNet project team, highlighted by successful procurement, design, engineering, and deployment of multiple classes of deployable assets. The JerseyNet deployable assets have already successfully deployed to support many in-state communications initiatives, as well as neighboring states' response efforts when required. Of special note, the project successfully supported the September 2015 Papal visit to Philadelphia using their System on Wheels (SOW) trailers and van and Sports Utility Vehicle (SUV)-based Vehicular Network Systems (VNS). The project also successfully supported concerts and other annual events in Atlantic City, multiple exercises validating the value of public-safety specific applications and network resources, and, most recently, support of the PGA Championship in Springfield, NJ.

Public safety agency use of the JerseyNet broadband network continues to increase. In the remainder of 2016, FirstNet anticipates that JerseyNet will attract a substantial population of public safety users and further exercise the Key Learning Conditions (KLCs) defined in their Spectrum Management Lease Agreement (SMLA) with FirstNet. These KLCs are:

1. Demonstration and documentation of the use and capabilities of rapidly deployable assets;

2. Conducting emergency management exercises and training activities with these deployable assets; and

3. Documenting best practice Network Operations Center (NOC) notification approaches, including trouble ticketing, prioritization, reporting, and ticket close-out.

The network as a whole will continue to evolve and grow with changing technology similar to a traditional commercial network. This was the vision of Congress, and FirstNet intends to work with its eventual partner to manage continual advancement of the network, devices, and services to meet ongoing public safety needs. Because the Act does not mandate that public safety entities use FirstNet services, FirstNet and our future partner will have to provide public safety a value proposition and competitive offerings, featuring the latest technology, including deployable systems like those in the JerseyNet system.

————

RESPONSE TO WRITTEN QUESTION SUBMITTED BY HON. JOE MANCHIN TO
MICHAEL POTH

Question. It is my understanding that in addition to FirstNet, any state that chooses to opt out and build its own radio access network is also required to reinvest any fees they collect back into the operation, maintenance, and improvement of the nationwide network. Although Congress intended to balance the goal of building a nationwide network with an opportunity for states to build their own, it certainly did not intend to create an incentive for states to opt out of FirstNet's network. However, it has been brought to my attention that there is still some debate about whether higher-density states that have opted out would be able to divert some fees into state general funds.

Could the panel clarify if both FirstNet and the states that have opted out are required to reinvest any fees they collect back into the network?

Does the panel believe states could divert surplus fees into state general funds under the authorizing language?

Answer. It is Congress' vision of bringing mission critical broadband capabilities to public safety in all of the Nation's 56 states and territories that drives FirstNet's work. The task that Congress has given the organization is vast, not only because it has never been accomplished before, but also because FirstNet is working with limited resources. Accordingly, based on the language and intent of the Act and in consideration of the funding mechanisms available, FirstNet has interpreted the Act to require that all revenues, including user/subscriber fees or fees from any public-private partnership, received by either FirstNet or a state that successfully assumes responsibility for radio access network deployment must be reinvested in the network. *See* Final Interpretations of Parts of the Middle Class Tax Relief and Job Creation Act of 2012, 80 Fed. Reg. 63504 (Oct. 20, 2015).

More specifically, while not subject to the requirements of the Administrative Procedure Act (5 U.S.C. Chapter 5), FirstNet conducted an open, public comment process on this matter to obtain input from stakeholders leading to final legal interpretations of the Act. *See id.* Through this open proceeding and with the support of a majority of commenters, FirstNet concluded that network revenue gained by an opt-out state must be reinvested in that state's RAN, and any excess revenue (beyond what is reasonably necessary to build, operate, maintain, or upgrade the state's RAN) must be reinvested into the nationwide network. This conclusion is based on Congress' directive to ensure the fiscal sustainability, and ultimately the success of the project, nationwide inclusive of rural areas.

RESPONSE TO WRITTEN QUESTIONS SUBMITTED BY HON. GARY PETERS TO MICHAEL POTH

Question 1. Nearly one-third of Michigan's population lives in non-urban areas, many of which lack reliable access to broadband. Cities and towns in these regions, especially in Northern Michigan and the Upper Peninsula, are popular tourist destinations and can multiply their populations during the high season. I am concerned that FirstNet, to date, has focused its planning and coordination efforts in areas with existing broadband coverage, rather than first working to fill the gap in areas with no reliable access.

What is FirstNet doing to address these rural gaps and assure that public safety officials in our Nation's most rural areas will have access to FirstNet's broadband network?

Answer. To accomplish its mission to ensure the establishment of a Nationwide Public Safety Broadband Network (NPSBN) that is self-sustainable, is re-capitalized, and meets rural deployment requirements, Congress provided FirstNet three fundamental tools: a one-time allocation of $7 billion generated from spectrum auctions held by the Federal Communications Commission (FCC), 20 MHz of spectrum in the 700 MHz band known as Band 14, and the authority to assess fees and enter into covered leasing agreements (CLAs) to monetize the excess capacity of Band 14 spectrum.

FirstNet recognizes that rural deployment of the NPSBN is a part of its mission and that rural coverage will be needed in Michigan's rural areas and throughout rural America. FirstNet aims to identify and improve rural coverage gaps for public safety throughout the deployment of the NPSBN and FirstNet's intended 25-year contract with the RFP awardee.

As part of its planning efforts, FirstNet has taken a number of actions to ensure rural deployment of the network, including: consulting with and collecting data from states and territories (including Michigan) to identify coverage needs and objectives, setting rural deployment milestones as an evaluating factor in FirstNet's RFP to deploy the NPSBN, and incorporating technical solutions to address coverage in rural areas (*e.g.,* deployable capabilities) as part of the RFP.

Consultation and Data Collection:

FirstNet has consulted with local, state/territory, tribal, and Federal public safety entities to ensure that the NPSBN is designed to meet the needs of public safety across the country. FirstNet has and will continue to work through the SPOCs to gather feedback from key stakeholders for reviewing its deployment plan.

FirstNet will deliver a state plan to each governor regarding FirstNet's plan to deploy the RAN within the state or territory. Throughout the development of our RFP, FirstNet sought firsthand, original data from the states to ensure that the information passed onto the vendor community was state driven with accurate, local information. The RFP that the vendor community bid on, was built with the data received to ensure that the states had significant input into the development of the NPSBN. The State data collection was also made available in whole to all potential bidders.

FirstNet requested the following information from the states:

1. Coverage: Identify desired coverage within the state or territory and proposed build out phases.

2. Users and Operational Areas: Gather information on the eligible user base and their respective operational areas.

3. Capacity Planning: Estimate current data usage today from typical users with indicators of potential growth.

4. Current Providers/Procurement: Identify current service providers and plans, procurement vehicles, and barriers to adoption.

5. State Plan Decision Process: Document the final state plan review process prior to submission to the Governor and any potential barriers/issues FirstNet should be aware of.

Rural as Evaluating Factor in the RFP:

The Act also requires that FirstNet meet substantial rural milestones in each phase of NPSBN deployment to ensure that deployment in rural parts of the country were achieved at a similar speed as urban deployment. *See* 47 U.S.C. § 1426(b)(3). In the RFP, offerors were asked to propose solutions to reach rural milestones using Band 14 spectrum. The proposals should follow these phases, where IOC is the Initial Operating Capacity, and FOC is the Final Operating Capacity.

RFP Solicitation No. D15PS00295—Section J, Attachment J–8 IOC/FOC Timeline

Phase	IOC–1 6 months from award	IOC–2 12 months	IOC–3 24 months	IOC–4 36 months	IOC–5 48 months	FOC 60 months
Substantial Rural Milestones		Achievement of 20% of Contractor's proposed Band 14 coverage	Achievement of 60% of Contractor's proposed Band 14 coverage	Achievement of 80% of Contractor's proposed Band 14 coverage	Achievement of 95% of Contractor's proposed Band 14 coverage	Achievement of 100% of Contractor's proposed Band 14 coverage

FirstNet is in the process of RFP evaluation, and will be evaluating offerors' proposals on their proposed rural coverage and how they intend to meet those milestones.

Question 2. Once built, will FirstNet facilitate opportunities for spectrum sharing with local governments so FirstNet's network can be leveraged to provide consumer broadband services, on a secondary basis, for purposes such as business development, education, and telemedicine?

Answer. FirstNet's enabling legislation limits access to network capacity on a secondary basis for non-public safety services to those entities that enter into a Covered Leasing Agreement (CLA) with FirstNet. A CLA results from a "public-private arrangement" (*i.e.,* not government to government) in which the secondary user agrees to construct, manage, or operate all or a portion of the nationwide public safety broadband network and in return is permitted to access network capacity on a secondary basis for non-public safety services. *See* 47 U.S.C. § 1428. Consequently, it is not permissible under the Act for FirstNet to enter into a CLA (*i.e.,* "spectrum sharing arrangement") directly with or provide access to a local government for secondary use of the spectrum for non-public safety services. Further, to the extent that a local government entity provides a public safety service that qualifies it as a public safety entity under the Act, such an entity would be able to receive services directly from FirstNet.

FirstNet also understands that Michigan has amended state law to allow for private entities to co-locate at state owned sites. This was a forward looking action and is applauded by FirstNet. In the future, FirstNet, along with the private sector entity that is selected through the procurement process, will continue to look for opportunities that would allow for the expansion and deployment of the network in a cost-effective manner that leverage new partnerships that may not exist today.

Question 3. Companies that provide products and services in areas such as public safety, defense, and cybersecurity could greatly benefit from having access to the FirstNet network for research and development work as a way to address operational and technical challenges in their fields.

Do you expect that interested companies will be able to work with FirstNet to test new products and services on the FirstNet network?

Answer. As indicated above, the Act limits the access to and use of the FirstNet network to (1) public safety entities and (2) secondary users that enter into a CLA with FirstNet to construct, manage, or operate all or a portion of the nationwide public safety broadband network.

With respect to researching and testing products and services, the Act provided the Public Safety Communications Research (PSCR) program with $300 million for research and to assist in "the development of standards, technologies, and applications to advance wireless public safety communications," including for use on the FirstNet network. [See 47 U.S.C. §§ 1443, 1457.] PSCR has begun an innovative set of prize competitions to spur innovation and technical research in these focus areas. For additional information regarding PSCR's schedule and priority areas for research, please contact PSCR.

Additionally, in the RFP, FirstNet asked offerors to propose certification and compliance mechanisms for devices, applications, and services that will run on the network. FirstNet is developing a laboratory in Boulder, CO that will supplement our partner's proposed certification processes in order to support the integrity of the network and build public safety's confidence in FirstNet's devices and services. For more information on this topic relative to devices, see the following FirstNet blog: Kameron Behnan, Tech Talk: Intro to FirstNet's Device Approval Process, (Apr. 4, 2016), available at *http://www.firstnet.gov/newsroom/blog/tech-talk-intro-firstnets-device-approval-process*

RESPONSE TO WRITTEN QUESTIONS SUBMITTED BY HON. JOE MANCHIN TO JEFFREY S. MCLEOD

Question 1. It is my understanding that in addition to FirstNet, any state that chooses to opt out and build its own radio access network is also required to reinvest any fees they collect back into the operation, maintenance, and improvement of the nationwide network. Although Congress intended to balance the goal of building a nationwide network with an opportunity for states to build their own, it certainly did not intend to create an incentive for states to opt out of FirstNet's network. However, it has been brought to my attention that there is still some debate about whether higher-density states that have opted out would be able to divert some fees into state general funds.

Could the panel clarify if both FirstNet and the states that have opted out are required to reinvest any fees they collect back into the network?

Answer. NGA does not have sufficient information to offer substantive answers.

Question 2. Does the panel believe states could divert surplus fees into state general funds under the authorizing language?

Answer. NGA does not have sufficient information to offer substantive answers.

RESPONSE TO WRITTEN QUESTIONS SUBMITTED BY HON. JOE MANCHIN TO GENERAL ARTHUR J. LOGAN

Question 1. It is my understanding that in addition to FirstNet, any state that chooses to opt out and build its own radio access network is also required to reinvest any fees they collect back into the operation, maintenance, and improvement of the nationwide network. Although Congress intended to balance the goal of building a nationwide network with an opportunity for states to build their own, it certainly did not intend to create an incentive for states to opt out of FirstNet's network. However, it has been brought to my attention that there is still some debate about whether higher-density states that have opted out would be able to divert some fees into state general funds.

Could the panel clarify if both FirstNet and the states that have opted out are required to reinvest any fees they collect back into the network?

Answer.

FirstNet

Sec.6208 (a-d) authorizes FirstNet to assess and collect fees, establish fee amounts and receive annual approval from NTIA as to the fees assessed and that such fees may only be assessed with the approval of NTIA. Part (d) of the section states: "Required Reinvestment of the Funds—The First Responder Network Authority *shall reinvest amounts received from the assessment of fees under this section in the nationwide public safety broadband network by using such funds only for constructing, maintaining, operating, or improving the network.*" (emphasis added).

By that language, FirstNet is required to reinvest back into the network any fees collected.

Opt-Out States:

Section 6302 (f) indicates if a State chooses to build its own radio access network, the State shall pay any user fees associated with State use of elements of the core network. Subparagraph (g) Prohibition, subsection (2) Rule of Construction states: *Any revenue gained by the State from such a leasing agreement shall be used only for constructing, maintaining, operating, or improving the radio access network of the State.*

The language of this section appears to contemplate that a State choosing to build its own RAN, upon approval of its alternative plan by the FCC, must still pay FirstNet for the use of the NPSBN and any revenue it *may* gain from a leasing agreement as part of any public-private partnership derived from its approved alternate plan shall be used *only for constructing, maintaining, operating or improving the radio access network of the State.*

Conclusion: The language in both sections requires that any fees generated, either by FirstNet or an Opt-Out State, must be reinvested back into the network.

Question 2. Does the panel believe states could divert surplus fees into state general funds under the authorizing language?

Answer. The intent of the legislation was to create a Nationwide Public Safety Broadband Network (NPSBN) to fully support the unique communications needs of first responders. FirstNet is charged with taking all actions necessary to ensure the building, deployment, and operation of the NPSBN. The language of the statute does provide states the opportunity to "opt-out" and build their own RAN if conditions under the law are met and their alternate plans are approved.

What is consistent is that neither FirstNet nor the States which may elect to "opt-out" may use any fees collected for anything other than *constructing, maintaining, operating or improving the radio access network.*

Nothing in the language of the statute indicates States should be able to divert surplus fees into their respective state's general fund.

RESPONSE TO WRITTEN QUESTIONS SUBMITTED BY HON. KELLY AYOTTE TO ANDREW KATSAROS

Question 1. As you highlighted in your testimony, FirstNet has a coverage challenge with "the geography of 56 jurisdictions . . . and the bulk of the population residing in about 5 percent of the U.S. land mass. The rest of the population resides in rural and wilderness settings." The enormous task of balancing costs and fees in densely populated areas versus sparsely populated areas is not going unnoticed in my home state of New Hampshire. Concerns remain that FirstNet's footprint will remain small and constrained to southern New Hampshire's more densely populated cities. Do you believe that FirstNet has a viable path forward to provide sufficient buildout in rural areas that would enable effective first responder communications?

Answer.

Short Answer

It is OIG's understanding that, as of August 26, 2016, FirstNet continues to develop, but has not yet finalized, a specific path forward for the Nationwide Public Safety Broadband Network (NPSBN) build-out of rural and non-rural areas. FirstNet and its yet-to-be selected vendor must still propose a viable, sufficient plan that enables effective first responder communications in rural areas.

Background

As of August 26, 2016, FirstNet has not finalized a specific path forward for the NPSBN build-out of rural and non-rural areas. The path forward will become clearer after (1) FirstNet selects a NPSBN build-out vendor through its Request for Proposals (RFP) process, which is expected by the end of calendar year 2016; and (2) States decide whether to opt-in or opt-out of the Radio Access Network (RAN) State Plans. After these decisions are made, FirstNet and its vendor will be able to better estimate costs and fees, which will allow it to develop a specific plan for the build-out and deployment in rural and non-rural areas.

"By law, FirstNet is responsible for working through the designated State points of contact to consult with states, local communities, tribal governments, and first responders to gather requirements for developing RAN . . . State Plans."[1] Accordingly, FirstNet has developed a consultation process to discuss and understand State's rural coverage needs and other priorities. It will be critical that States communicate their needs during the consultation process and that FirstNet addresses those needs, especially during the development of RAN State Plans.

---

[1] National Telecommunications and Information Administration. "The Process for Working with FirstNet." See *https://www.ntia.doc.gov/files/ntia/publications/fact_sheet_process-9-19-13.pdf* (accessed August 31, 2016).

The Middle Class Tax Relief and Job Creation Act of 2012 (the Act) states that the nationwide network shall require deployment phases with substantial rural coverage milestones as part of each phase of the construction and deployment of the network. To the maximum extent economically desirable, such proposals shall include partnerships with existing commercial mobile providers to utilize cost-effective opportunities to speed deployment in rural areas.[2]

Consistent with the Act, FirstNet established substantial rural milestones in its RFP that require coverage in rural areas in each phase of the build-out. FirstNet will also evaluate potential vendors on a variety of factors, including the vendor's capability of providing rural coverage. For example, FirstNet will evaluate, in part, a potential vendor's capability of providing coverage and capacity in each of the 56 States and territories, including rural and non-rural areas. In addition, FirstNet will evaluate potential vendors "based on their demonstration of their existing and planned partnerships with rural telecommunications providers, including commercial mobile providers, utilizing existing infrastructure to the maximum extent economically desirable to speed deployment in rural areas."[3]

Question 2. Additionally, how can FirstNet provide cost certainty and transparent billing to states with concerns that there will be unforeseen costs—especially that buildout to rural areas may fall on their shoulders?

Answer.

Short Answer

Although FirstNet has made progress in establishing the NPSBN, OIG believes it is too early for FirstNet to be able to provide cost certainty and transparent billing to States and territories.

Background

Public safety entity (PSE) NPSBN user cost is dependent on FirstNet's upcoming selection of a vendor to partner with on the design, build, and implementation of the NPSBN. "In January 2016, FirstNet issued a RFP for the purpose of seeking a vendor to build and operate the NPSBN."[4] Included within the RFP is an objective to "[e]stablish (i) compelling, differentiated, and competitively priced service packages and (ii) sales, distribution, and marketing capabilities to ensure adoption of FirstNet products and services by a majority of eligible PSEs within four years of award."[5] Since PSEs are not required to subscribe to FirstNet services, the pricing schedule developed by FirstNet and its contracted vendor will affect whether PSEs choose to subscribe to FirstNet services. FirstNet plans to award the contract by the end of calendar year 2016.

Additionally, State decisions regarding whether to opt-in or opt-out of FirstNet's NPSBN will affect the cost of using FirstNet's core network. Following the award of the contract, FirstNet is required to provide States with a plan that describes its approach to provide NPSBN coverage in the State. To obtain the information necessary to develop State Plans, FirstNet has consulted with—and requested information from—States and territories.

Under the Act, Governors will be given the opportunity to review the FirstNet-provided State Plan to determine if it meets the State's needs.[6] If a State decides to opt-in, FirstNet will be responsible for deploying, operating, and upgrading the RAN in that State, including getting PSEs to purchase its service. If a State decides that the plan does not meet its PSE needs and opts-out, the State can then deploy its own RAN by providing an alternative plan to the Federal Communications Commission (FCC) and National Telecommunications and Information Administration (NTIA) for approval and by negotiating a spectrum lease agreement with FirstNet to tie into the NPSBN core network. Under this option, the State would determine the build-out to rural areas, associated prices to PSEs, and related costs.

FirstNet has acknowledged the challenges of balancing costs and fees from densely populated areas versus sparsely populated areas. In considering network funding and revenue reinvestment provisions, FirstNet noted that

---

[2] See *Middle Class Tax Relief and Job Creation Act of 2012 (The Act)*, Pub. L. No. 112–96, § 6206(b)(3), 126 Stat. 212.

[3] U.S. Department of the Interior, Interior Business Center, January 13, 2016. *FirstNet Nationwide Public Safety Broadband Network (NPSBN)*, Solicitation Number: D15PS00295. Herndon, VA: DOI, Sect M, M–2.

[4] U.S. Department of Commerce Office of Inspector General, June 21, 2016. *Ongoing Activities and Challenges Facing the First Responder Network Authority in their Establishment of a Nationwide Public Safety Broadband Network*, OIG–16–034–T. Washington, DC: DOC OIG, 2.

[5] DOI Interior Business Center, January 13, 2016. *FirstNet Nationwide Public Safety Broadband Network (NPSBN)*, Solicitation Number: D15PS00295E. Herndon, VA: DOI, Section C.

[6] See *Middle Class Tax Relief and Job Creation Act of 2012 (The Act)*, Pub. L. No. 112–96, § 6302(e)(2), 126 Stat. 219–220.

Congress mandated that FirstNet deploy a self-sustaining, nationwide network, irrespective of if a State opts-in or opts-out. Given the finite funding sources and Congress' mandate that FirstNet meet substantial rural milestones, it is critical that FirstNet leverages the high-density, high-revenue-generating areas of all States. This nationwide solution achieves expeditious delivery of dedicated, wireless broadband services to public safety in all areas of the country.[7]

As it must meet the massive costs of deploying the nationwide network, FirstNet has stated that it has a duty to protect the fees generated in high-density areas in excess of what is needed to reasonably maintain the RAN for use in building-out rural coverage areas.[8]

Question 3. Lastly, what do you believe are the most important aspects for states to consider when deciding whether to opt-in or opt-out of FirstNet's proposal?

Answer.

Short Answer

When deciding whether to opt-in or opt-out of FirstNet's proposal for an individual State or territory, governors of States and territories must weigh how well the provided State Plan meets their public safety needs against the responsibilities (deploying, operating, and upgrading) and accompanying risks associated with deploying the State RAN on their own.

Background

Consistent with the Act, FirstNet will provide a State Plan to governors so they can decide whether FirstNet (opt-in) or the State/territory (opt-out) takes on the responsibility to deploy, operate, and maintain the RAN that will interconnect with the nationwide core network. This decision has serious implications in terms of the responsibilities and accompanying risks a State will assume, including:

- For opt-in entities, no additional action is needed as FirstNet provides funds to deploy, operate, and upgrade the network for that State or territory.
- For opt-out entities, States and territories are responsible for funding the network deployment (with potential grant money), operation, and maintenance. If this option is selected, States and territories must develop an alternative plan to be approved by the FCC and obtain NTIA approval that the plan meets the requirements of the Act (*e.g.,* ongoing interoperability, cost effectiveness, and comparable security, coverage, timeliness, and quality of service). States and territories would then need to negotiate a spectrum capacity lease with FirstNet.

To facilitate the development of responsive State Plans, FirstNet has conducted ongoing efforts such as initial consultations, State data submissions, public notices, and governance body meetings to capture the needs and wishes of local, State, and tribal public safety stakeholders. FirstNet will provide State Plan information related to (1) extent of coverage; (2) services (*e.g.,* plans, pricing, and security); (3) applications and features; and (4) devices and accessories to be considered in deciding whether to opt-in or opt-out. As FirstNet has acknowledged in its June 21, 2016 testimony before this Committee, the goal of getting to 100 percentage of coverage throughout the 56 States and territories is aggressive; we believe coverage, particularly in rural areas, to be a key variable in each State's decision.

RESPONSE TO WRITTEN QUESTIONS SUBMITTED BY HON. JOE MANCHIN TO
ANDREW KATSAROS

Question 1. It is my understanding that in addition to FirstNet, any state that chooses to opt out and build its own radio access network is also required to reinvest any fees they collect back into the operation, maintenance, and improvement of the nationwide network. Although Congress intended to balance the goal of building a nationwide network with an opportunity for states to build their own, it certainly did not intend to create an incentive for states to opt out of FirstNet's network. However, it has been brought to my attention that there is still some debate about whether higher-density states that have opted out would be able to divert some fees into state general funds.

---

[7] FirstNet. "FirstNet Network Funding and Revenue Reinvestment Provisions." See *http:// www.firstnet.gov/sites/default/files/FirstNet-Network-Funding-Revenue-Reinvestment-Provisions.pdf* (accessed August 31, 2016).

[8] FirstNet, September 2015. "Use of State and Local Infrastructure, Rural Coverage, 'Early Builders' and Pilots, Frequently Asked Questions (FAQs)." Page 2. See *http://www.firstnet.gov/ sites/default/files/Use%20of%20local-state-infrastructure%20FAQs__150902.pdf* (accessed August 31, 2016).

Could the panel clarify if both FirstNet and the states that have opted out are required to reinvest any fees they collect back into the network?

Answer.

Short Answer

Our understanding is that both the First Responder Network Authority (FirstNet) and the States that opt out are required to reinvest excess fees back into the network.

Background

The Middle Class Tax Relief and Job Creation Act of 2012 (the Act) authorizes FirstNet to be a permanent self-funding entity, assessing and collecting network user fees, lease fees related to network capacity, and lease fees related to network equipment and infrastructure.[1] The Act states that the total amount of fees assessed for each Fiscal Year shall be sufficient, and not exceed the amount necessary, to recoup the total expenses of FirstNet in carrying out its duties and responsibilities.[2] FirstNet must reinvest amounts received from the assessment of fees in the Nationwide Public Safety Broadband Network (NPSBN) by using such funds only for constructing, maintaining, operating, or improving the network.[3]

The Act further requires that those States that wish to opt out of FirstNet and build their own Radio Access Network (RAN) to submit their alternative plans for the RAN to the Federal Communications Commission (FCC). Upon approval of the plan by the FCC, the States are required to apply to the National Telecommunications and Information Administration (NTIA) to lease spectrum capacity from FirstNet.[4] Those States must demonstrate the cost-effectiveness of their alternative plans, among other requirements.[5] FirstNet, as the designated licensee of the spectrum and an independent authority within NTIA, must ultimately decide the terms for entering into spectrum capacity leases and whether to enter into a lease with a State.[6] Similar to FirstNet requirements, the Act states that "[a]ny revenue gained by the State from such a leasing agreement shall be used only for constructing, maintaining, operating, or improving the radio access network of the State."[7]

FirstNet has published its *Final Interpretations of Parts of the Middle Class Tax Relief and Job Creation Act of 2012* in the Federal Register.[8] Below, we highlight FirstNet's interpretations that indicate States will be required to reinvest fees back into the NPSBN.

FirstNet explained that it "has an obligation to ensure the establishment of a nationwide network and must take into consideration the interests of all States rather than only a single State."[9] FirstNet then determined that "as a part of its decision to enter into a spectrum capacity lease it must take into account the cost-effectiveness of the proposed alternative State plan, including the impact of the plan on the nationwide network."[10]

FirstNet concluded that as part of the cost-effective analysis in determining whether and under what terms to enter into a spectrum capacity lease, it "may require that amounts generated within a State in excess of those required to reasonably sustain the State RAN, be utilized to support the Act's requirement to deploy the NPSBN on a nationwide basis."[11] FirstNet also concluded that the Act requires opt-out States—*i.e.,* ones that assume the responsibilities for RAN deployment and charge user fees—to reinvest such fees into the network.[12] Finally, FirstNet concluded that, as part of its cost-effectiveness analysis, it must consider State reinvestment and distribution of any user fees assessed to public safety entities or spectrum capacity revenues in determining whether and under what terms to enter into a spectrum capacity lease.[13]

---

[1] See *Middle Class Tax Relief and Job Creation Act of 2012 (The Act)*, Pub. L. No. 112–96, § 6208(a), 126 Stat. 215–16.

[2] *Id. at* § 6208(b), 126 Stat. 216.

[3] *Id. at* § 6208(d), 126 Stat. 216.

[4] *Id. at* § 6302(e)(3), 126 Stat. 220–21.

[5] *Id. at* § 6302(e)(3)(D), 126 Stat. 220–21.

[6] *Final Interpretations of Parts of the Middle Class Tax Relief and Job Creation Act of 2012,* 80 Fed. Reg. 63,504, 63519 (Oct. 20, 2015).

[7] *The Act,* Pub. L. No. 112–96 § 6302(g)(2), 126 Stat. 221.

[8] 80 Fed. Reg. 63,504 (Oct. 20, 2015).

[9] *Id.* at 63,520

[10] *Ibid.*

[11] *Id.* at 63,519.

[12] *Id.* at 63,506.

[13] *Id.* at 63,519.

FirstNet, in making its final interpretation regarding its analyzing funding considerations as part of its determination to enter into a spectrum capacity lease, stated that:

> States seeking and receiving approval of alternative RAN plans could materially affect FirstNet's funding sources and thus its ability to serve public safety, particularly in rural States. More precisely, a State that assumes RAN deployment responsibilities could benefit from, or supplant, these funding sources by generating and retaining amounts in excess of that necessary to reasonably maintain the particular State RAN through monetization of FirstNet's licensed spectrum. By doing so, the excess value above that reasonably needed to operate and maintain the RAN would no longer be available to help ensure that nationwide deployment, particularly in higher cost rural areas, will occur. This undermines the intent of the Act and the express requirement for FirstNet to deploy in rural areas as part of each phase of implementation.[14]

Accordingly, FirstNet concludes, based on the language and intent of the Act that Congress did not intend to permit alternative RAN plans that inefficiently utilize scarce spectrum resources to hinder the nationwide deployment of the NPSBN by depriving it of needed financial support. FirstNet further concludes that it must thus consider the effect of any such material inefficiencies, among other things, on the NPSBN in determining whether and what terms to enter into a spectrum capacity lease.[15]

Question 2. Does the panel believe states could divert surplus fees into state general funds under the authorizing language?

Answer. Based on our response to the previous question, we do not believe States are able to divert surplus fees into State general funds under the authorizing language and FirstNet's interpretations.

○

---

[14] *Id.* at 63,518–19.
[15] *Id.* at 63,519.

57

This page intentionally left blank.

58

This page intentionally left blank.

59

This page intentionally left blank.